Testimoı

I have just finished **Step Up**. *I feel humbled, hopeful and connected. It is beautiful. It is everything the universities don't have and more. It's stunning, radiant, exhilarating, profound, and contains so much of what I've been searching for all my life. May Allah help more women to tap into their inner wisdom, intuition and strength that God has blessed us all with, with this insightful, vulnerable, and truly compassionate book.* **– Janine Allison Hood, Australia**

Wow! Loved every bit of it! I was gripped from the beginning to the end. It was so raw, authentic and super inspiring. I loved the way you take the reader along your personal journey, at the same time stay[ing] connected with [the] reality of life. It makes one think and reflect on themselves. Kathryn, your courage, passion and heartfelt words shine through as a true leader. May Allah (swt) reward you infinitely and make it a huge success! **– Robina Kauser, Inside Out Relationship Coach, UK**

The worst enemy you could ever have in life is yourself. I found it hard to love myself and blamed everyone around me for everything that was wrong in my life. When I joined Kathryn, I learnt and began to understand [that] feelings come from thought in the moment. I realised how much power I had within myself. This new understanding has given me a new lens to see my life with. I am in a place of peace – from darkness into light – in tune with the reality of how things really are as I continue to learn and understand deeper and see life with more clarity. You can really be peaceful inside out. **– Sajida Sacranie, Peaceful Parenting Leader, Ireland**

Working with Kathryn was the best investment I made in myself last year. Not only did it strengthen my relationship to Allah, it also helped me increase in self-confidence. I feel deeply transformed, and have grown in Tawakkul (putting trust in Allah), authenticity and self-awareness. I'm so grateful I was able to take part of this as it has helped me going through the storms of life much more peacefully. **– Maryline David, Ireland**

Working with Kathryn has transformed my life with profound shifts in my thinking. I have been able to be so present, calm and connected to Allah that it feels it's just Him and me. So I can conquer any challenge that comes my way. I feel His guidance in every step I take with full confidence. That means not having the fears I did before of people and circumstances and that there are no limits except the ones I put on myself. Kathryn's leadership and dynamics of the support group have brought me closer than I ever imagined to my Creator. I've been her student for over two years and am so grateful Allah brought us together. **– Rayesa Gheewala, High Performance Coach, USA**

This understanding has increased my self-awareness and has improved all my relationships. I am more tolerant and compassionate towards others (especially my husband). I have acquired flexibility when it comes to understanding other people. I have been able to forgive and forget difficult past issues I had with people. **– Romy Ramos, Parenting Coach, Australia**

The effect of everything I learned from Kathryn is with me everyday. Not just influencing my relationships with my kids, especially Musa, but also my whole family. **– Umm Musa, Australia**

Step Up

Embrace the Leader Within

Kathryn Jones

First published in 2018

ISBN:
Print: 978-1-925692-97-6
Ebook: 978-1-925692-50-1

Edited and Published by Busybird Publishing
Cover image: Busybird Publishing
Cover design Busybird Publishing
Layout and typesetting: WorkingType Studio
Typeset in Proxima Nova

Busybird Publishing
2/118 Para Road
Montmorency Victoria
Australia 3094

To all Muslim women.

May this be a reminder to us all,
including myself first.

The implications of the Inside Out Paradigm and how I explain them have been greatly influenced by this work:

Implications NOT Applications

This is the unpublished work of Keith Blevens PhD and Valda Munroe. Their work can be found at:

https://threeprinciplesparadigm.com

I ask Allah to reward my sisters in Islam who dedicated their time to reading and giving me feedback throughout my journey of writing this book. Thanks also to Professor Mohamad Abdulla who took time out of his vacation to revise this book, make some valuable suggestions and verify that my interpretations of Islamic references were sound.

BONUS

DOWNLOAD THE AUDIOBOOK FREE!

Read this first!

Just to say thanks for buying my book, I would like to give you the Audiobook version 100% FREE!

To download go to:

www.StepUpBonus.com

Contents

Foreword

Our life experiences and the people in our lives can either make us or break us. Like many other survivors of trauma, I made the choice to step up and transform my hardships into a force that benefits humanity. My struggles could have broken me completely, and I admit there are pieces of my life that I cannot put back together, nor do I want to. Instead, my struggles made me who I am today, and even though it's painful, I am grateful.

I met Kathryn when she invited me to speak on her inaugural Me First Summit. Kathryn was aware of the work that I did educating women to overcome pelvic health issues, and she wanted me to share my message with the beautiful Muslim women she worked with. Kathryn knew that many women did not prioritise their health, especially their pelvic floor health after children and their hormonal health.

I loved the concept of 'Me First' and it really resonated with me. Throughout my entire life, I don't think I ever really practiced putting myself first. I was always the 'carer', the 'giver', the 'rescuer' and I spent most of my life trying to save others. Even today, the work that I do through my business The Pelvic Expert is focused on helping others, however I now have systems and processes in place so that I don't drain my own cup whilst trying to fill the cups of others.

'Verily, with every hardship comes ease' – such a powerful verse from the Qur'an, and one that I have branded in my heart. I believe Allah has tested me with my hardships so that I may use them to help other women feel ease. And that itself is not an easy thing to do. In these pages, Kathryn eloquently shows how her own extreme hardships have shaped her and inspired her to become the leader that she is for other women.

Perhaps you notice that you have been neglecting your own self-care, living to serve others, or perhaps you've been feeling stuck or uninspired. In this book, Kathryn shares in very intimate detail her own journey to inspired leadership, within herself, as a Muslim woman, as a parent, as a business-woman, and, most inspiringly, as a leader for other Muslim women. It takes a lot of courage for a Muslim woman to open up and share the pains of the past, and I commend her unabashed fearlessness.

Like Kathryn, I was bullied and oppressed throughout my childhood. I lived in a constant state of fear, anxiety and depression. I was surrounded by narcis-sistic and psychopathic personalities. My childhood was filled with emotional abuse, verbal abuse, physical abuse, spiritual abuse and narcissistic abuse. When Kathryn wrote about walking on eggshells in her marriage, that remind-ed me of how I felt all through my childhood.

I once read a story about a Muslim man who was unjustly imprisoned. He was complaining to his friend about how his life was revolving around this trial. His friend shared some very powerful insights which I have never for-gotten. He shared that many of us have a theme in life that Allah has cho-sen for us, and our lives circle around these themes and patterns, similar to how the universe has circular patterns. The Earth orbits around the sun, which orbits around the Milky Way. Muslims orbit around the Ka'bah, when we pray and when we make Tawaf. Electrons orbit around the nucleus of the atom, and so on.

For example, Prophet Yusuf (AS) had the theme of his shirt, which his life circled around. When he was thrown in the well, his brothers brought back his shirt stained with blood to their father to show he had been eaten by a wolf. When his master's wife tried to seduce him, his shirt was used to explain that she had grabbed him from behind. In the end, Yusuf (AS) sends his shirt with his brothers to their father to prove that he is still alive, and this restores his father's eyesight. We see a similar theme of water for Prophet Musa (AS).

For me, it's no surprise that the theme of my life is the 'pelvis'. From a young age, I suffered from bladder and bowel problems. I lived in such a state

2

of stress and fear, in 'fight or flight' on a daily basis, that my body rarely entered the opposing state of 'rest and digest'. I would be so constipated that I would only visit the bathroom once a week. In my teens, I suffered from horrendous period pain, only to be diagnosed with endometriosis in my early twenties.

When I entered the workforce, I injured my pelvis so badly that I couldn't walk without crutches for months and my right leg muscles atrophied to half their size. My nerves were on fire and I was in chronic pelvic pain for many years after this. In my pregnancy I had such horrible pubic pain that I couldn't get out of bed without screaming. Today, I am the founder of The Pelvic Expert, and I help other women with pelvic problems, from pain to bladder leakage to constipation and more, overcome them.

After reading Kathryn's book, I wonder if the theme of her life is abuse. She writes many stories of various forms of oppression she faced. And she embraced the leadership within herself to now help other women who have faced abuse and oppression. She teaches Peaceful Parenting so that we do not continue to perpetuate the cycle and abuse or oppress our own children. She teaches self-care, and putting yourself first, so that we don't abuse or oppress ourselves. And she creates business leaders, so that women can take charge and break free of financial abuse.

Perhaps you are aware of a theme or a pattern in your life. It could be failed relationships, sicknesses, poverty, war or it could be abuse. There does seem to be a cycle with abuse. I know that my own abusers were abused. Some of us, like Kathryn, go on to marry abusers. Others become abusers themselves. Abusers make the choice to perpetuate the cycle, abusing their own and others.

I made the choice to cut ties with my abusers, and anyone who made excuses for them, or 'enablers'. And in doing so, I was able to really embrace my leadership, just as Kathryn did. You have a choice to let your experiences hold you down. Or you can step up and change your life, find your purpose and lead others to the same.

Consider that theme in your life, and then consider your purpose in life. I belief purpose is the happy middle of passion, mission, vocation and profession. To find your passion, think about what you are good at and what you love. To find your mission, think about what you love and what the world needs. To find your vocation, think about what the world needs and what you can be paid for. To find your profession, think about what you can be paid for and what you are good at.

Having a purpose in life allows us to be hopeful, to shape our futures and to strive for excellence. That purpose has to be in line with spirituality. Allah puts tests in our lives, but these are actually opportunities. There is always something that can be learnt from these testing hardships. They are opportunities for spiritual growth, personal growth and professional growth.

Sometimes the toxicity of our childhoods or our intimate relationships or our school or work environments can continue to shackle us. Sometimes our past becomes our present as we live and relive painful memories, finding excuses to keep those proverbial shackles on so that we don't break free to live a hopeful future. Sometimes those outside voices become our own inside voices, and we become our own worst enemy.

If you're reading this book, you're listening to that growing voice in your heart that is calling out for you to step up. We all have the capacity within ourselves to be empowered, to be leaders in all aspects of our lives, and for some of us that staircase can be steep. But as they say: every journey begins with a single step.

Along the way, you will have to wave goodbye to those parts of yourself that hold you back, and banish the negative self-talk. You will have to push away those toxic people, and hold strong so as not to allow them to walk back into your life. In this book, through her own experiences and insights, Kathryn will reach out her hand and help lead you to take the first step. Sometimes she will give you that nudge from behind when you feel yourself taking a step backwards, but most of the journey she will walk beside you, until you reach your destination, stronger, empowered, confident, embracing the leader within.

Every one of us has free will, even if you don't believe that right now. We all have the power to make a choice about what we do and how we feel. We can choose to be victims of our trauma, or we can take a page out of Kathryn's book, and make the bold choice, to step up to the winner's podium and become victors. We can step up, embrace the leader within, and lead others to victory.

Heba Shaheed
The Pelvic Expert

Introduction

Why?

> *'No problem can be solved from the same level of consciousness that created it.' – Albert Einstein*

My forehead rested heavily on the prayer mat, soaked by the flood of tears.

What can I do?

Worn down, beaten, empty.

It was just me, Allah and my pain.

The years of abuse had taken their toll on me physically, emotionally and spiritually. I had even had the passing thought that I would be so much better off if I just closed my eyes and slipped away in the night. I was tired. I didn't want to try anymore. I just didn't have the strength.

It was midway through Ramadan in 2002 when I had that thought. I was four months pregnant. My 18-month-old son and I were really ill and all he would take was my milk.

It was expected that there would be hot, freshly prepared meals at 3.30am for Suhor (the pre-dawn meal in Ramadan). I was aggressively roused from sleep and made to serve the family on the one night I had prepared everything for them in advance.

It was the words of my doctor, who had witnessed my declining mental and physical state, that snapped me out of my daze. 'Who will look after your kids?' she asked. Thus began six weeks of crying into my prayer mat asking Allah for the answer.

In that moment, I stepped back into being the leader I have always been and began a long, hard journey out of my marriage to the place I am today. Alhamdu Lillah (praise be to Allah).

> *'Being a candle is not easy: in order to give light one must first burn.' – Rumi*

When I look back at the person who left that marriage, and then back further to the tribulations of my childhood, I truly believe that I have been on a life-long boot camp to prepare me for what I am doing today. So many women are suffering, oppressed and exhausted from the constant struggle. They need to see that it is possible to live with fearless confidence, resilience and inner peace. It is my hope that this book will be a candle for Muslim women – for any woman – to be the light at the end of the dark tunnel, guiding them in the right direction, insha Allah (God willing).

I began the book with a quote from Einstein – 'No problem can be solved from the same level of consciousness that created it' – because it is time to raise the consciousness of Muslim women to realise and embrace the gifts that Allah blessed them with so they can live purposefully in this life.

It is also time to raise the consciousness of how the world views Muslim women so they can be seen as the gift they are to the world.

Across the globe atrocities are being committed. Daily, the news is filled with hate, terror, war, murder and the like. In an effort to dehumanise a fifth of the human race the spotlight is on Muslims. The language to describe atrocities committed by Muslims is tailored to paint a picture that suits those who wish to control by fear. It is the Muslim women who bear the brunt of such rhetoric. Visible by the scarf she wears on her head she becomes the target of hatred.

As a white, Anglo-Saxon Australian whose family migrated here in the 1830s and 1840s, Australia is the only country I have ever called home. Yet I hear the words 'Go back to where you came from', am lectured about how 'lucky' I am that the Australian Government is helping me, have the word 'terrorist' muttered at me as a shopper passes me in the supermarket and am 'randomly' tested for bomb residue in every airport.

This was not my experience in 1995 when I embraced Islam. People were genuinely curious about why I wore a scarf and felt safe to just ask about it. I was often told how well I spoke English, but there was no hatred behind their eyes, just genuine curiosity.

Since September 11, 2001, this has all changed.

When old ladies almost knock cans from shelves to steer their trolley away from me in the supermarket with an expression of terror on their face because news outlets have shown awful pictures of what some so-called Australian Muslim convert has done overseas, it breaks my heart that I no longer belong in my own country.

When a seven-year-old in my son's class tells him he doesn't belong in Australia because he is Muslim, it breaks my heart to see the confusion and pain on his face.

When I see my children, who are eighth generation Australian from my side of the family, feeling like they don't belong in Australian society because a few people in the world decided that Muslims are the scapegoat for world dominance, I just want to pack up and leave!

That's when I knew I had to use the gifts I have been blessed with to be part of the solution.

It's time for me to be the leader I am and help lead Muslim women to be a powerful part of the solution simply by being their beautiful selves in their best form. We are the most visible; let people see through us who Muslims are and what Islam is really about.

It's time for us to be the role models for our children so they feel it is safe to hold their heads high and be whom they truly are.

It's just time!

The concept of leadership in this book is all encompassing. It is for every woman, no matter what her circumstances.

This is an invitation for my sisters in Islam to join me in discovering the amazing women who preceded us and how inspiring their lives were. To learn what it is that might be holding them back from living a fulfilled and purposeful life. And, most of all, to venture into the Inside Out Paradigm with me and see just how possible it is for them to live their life with fear-less courage, resilience and inner peace.

Most of all, it is to guide them to embracing the natural leader that is inside each and every one of them.

I also invite anyone who feels that Muslim women are oppressed by the religion of Islam to venture into these pages and discover the truth.

‘Everyone shines given the right lighting.’ – Susan Cain

May Allah make this book a shining light and accept it from me as my gratitude for the blessings He has bestowed upon me.

The next few pages are poems I wrote as I was recovering from domestic violence. I was alone in my journey, so pen and paper became my company in those moments when it felt uncomfortable to be in my own skin.

Sailing the Seas of Violence

The wedding ship sails into the sunset.
Pink ripples meet the horizon,
As the hull parts the water like a knife through soft butter.
The gentle breeze flapping the flags.
The rolling of the boat, soothing.
Not a cloud in sight.
Not a hint of unrest.

So the journey continues.
Slight rises in the swell roll the ship.
Side to side.
Back and forth.
Slightly unsettling,
But it passes.

Then some clouds cut across the sun's rays.
Darkening the voyage.
And they pass.

The sun is shining.
The sea like a mirror, reflecting its brightness.
It is again blissful.
Swells and darkness forgotten.
Just a dream.

But it is not.
The swells grow.
The clouds grow darker.
The calms less frequent.

Now the storm is really brewing.
There is thunder.

Plenty of thunder.
Thunder all around.
Louder.
And passes.

Again there is calm, but it is broken by uncertainty.
The sun rays now burn, not glisten.
There is a sickening feeling in the air.

It doesn't last.

The thunder roars again.
Now the lightening precedes it with force.
The ship thrashes against the waves.
Crashing back and forth.
Battered.
Sails flapping frantically against the gale force winds.

The sea is angry.
Grey.
Peeking waves coming from all directions.
No rest between assaults against the ship's bow.
No warning from which direction.
The ship powerless to the onslaught.

Just as quickly as it came,
The storm disappears.
The sky opens.
The clouds parting to let the sun sparkle through.

The ship still.
Dishevelled.
Wrecked.

The sea gently massages its hull.
The sun caresses the deck.
Promises anew.

Possibly hope.

But the hull creaks under the pressure of the damage.
The sail flaps, torn and ragged.
The ship rolls on the sea in anticipation.
The anchor dragging in the sand below,
As if pleading with the vessel to sail to safer waters.

Night falls.
A new day begins.
Night falls again.

Calm and rest.
False hope rising.

It started with a hint of rain.
A few specks hit the deck.

The swell rises.
Dark clouds rush the sky.
Winds wail through the riggings.

Not again.

The thrashing against the vicious waves.
The bombardment of water across the deck.
The bouncing from one wave crest to another, then crashing down again.

It is too much.

The hull begins to crack.

The water swallows the ship,
Sending it to the depths of the sea.

*Just as the ship was not responsible for the weather,
you are not responsible for their behaviour.*

*You can however listen to the anchor and sail
to calmer waters.*

Am I Going Crazy?

I love you.
You are the light of my life.
I adore you.
He loves me.

It's all your fault.
You are useless.
Can't you do anything right?
He loves me not.

Sweet heart.
Honey.
Sweetness.
He loves me.

You wicked woman.
Get lost.
I regret marrying you.
He loves me not.

My beloved wife.
You are a joy to behold.
What beauty lies in your eyes.
He loves me.

Wench.
You disgust me.
You have no right!
He loves me not.

I love you so much that …
I love you but …

loves me
not
loves me
not

How can I love someone who destroys my spirit as a woman?
Whose every word and action
confuses me
zaps me of self esteem
and leaves me
hollow
afraid
stressed
unsure
lost
helpless
used
and most of all **NOT ME**.

This is not love.

This is CONTROL.

Chapter 1

Who Are These Women?

When I first embraced Islam in 1995 I didn't know any Muslim women at all. In fact, my desire to become a Muslim came purely from reading the Qur'an on my own, not through any influence of a Muslim at that time. It was my own personal journey.

I met a Muslim who introduced me to Islam, shared with me a video by Keith Moore discussing verses of the Qur'an that described the development of the embryo and had given me a copy of the Qur'an before heading back to his home country. I wanted to read the verses Keith Moore had mentioned but I hadn't written them down anywhere and I couldn't find embryology in the index, so I decided to start reading the Qur'an from the beginning.

One morning in October I woke up and I just knew in my heart that I was going to become a Muslim that day. There isn't any explanation other than that it was Allah's guidance, Alhamdu Lillah (praise be to Allah). I don't recall where I was up to in the Qur'an. It wasn't a particular verse, story or message; it was purely a sense of belief and commitment that this was the path for me.

When I embraced Islam, my knowledge of Islam was really limited. It came from what I'd read in the pages of the Qur'an. I didn't have much idea what it would mean to my life moving forward, I just knew in my heart it was exactly what I needed to do.

I strongly believed and I wanted to be a Muslim.

Usually, when you enter a new phase in your life, it's as a result of seeing someone else and wanting to be like them – having a role model, a mentor, even a coach. In this particular case, I had no one around me, no Muslim women at all that were there to guide me or show me the way.

I was left to figure it out for myself and as Allah says in the Qur'an:

Do the people think that they will be left to say, 'We believe' and they will not be tried? – Qur'an (29:2)

My first test started immediately.

The person I had contacted to help me become a Muslim decided to take me under his wing. I was unaware that his behaviour with me was not acceptable in Islam because, throughout my life, I had many male friends and studied and worked in male dominant fields. So being alone with a man was not something that alerted me to the fact that there was issue in his practise of Islam.

I was genuine in my intent, but also very vulnerable through my lack of knowledge. He continued to spend time with me and tell me how knowledgeable he was in Islam and how fortunate I was to have him to teach me. I believed him. I fell into the trap of a narcissistic and abusive person who took advantage of my lack of knowledge to convince me that the best decision for me to be a good Muslim was to marry him.

That was the beginning of many, many years of social isolation. Not knowing any Muslim women. Not having any close Muslim friends at all. I didn't have role models. The version of Islam that I was learning was from his distorted views on how men and women are meant to interact.

In fact, for the first eight years of being a Muslim, I was subjected to a life of financial, social, spiritual, sexual, verbal, emotional and physical abuse.

I knew deep down in my heart that it wasn't right. There was something that didn't fit, but I didn't have access to the knowledge I needed back then to be able to know any different. It was difficult to get hold of books. It was the early days of the Internet (we had dialup back then). You could find some articles, but it was very hard to know what was good and bad about what was out there. Any time I ordered a book he would tell me not to read it because it would corrupt me because it had weak references here and there. He made sure I didn't have access to anything or anyone who could show me what Islam was really about!

Knowledge of Islam and this beautiful way of life is empowering! Knowing what Allah and His Messenger (peace be upon him) really said about women in Islam and their rights, roles and responsibilities frees us to lead a life that is purposeful and fulfilling

Then learning about the amazing Muslim women predecessors, the wives and the female companions of the Prophet (peace be upon him), I realised that what I intuitively knew was right was actually the way it was meant to be in Islam. Not this crazy version of Islam I had been taught by my husband since I embraced Islam.

This is why it's so important that we know our role models. That we know about their lives, their stories and the amazing things that they did. That we know what Islam says about us as Muslim women from a reliable source. So we can confidently stand up for our rights, fulfil our responsibilities and be the best role models ourselves for those who follow us!

So, who are these women?

Aisha Bint Abu Bakr is the first woman that I wish to introduce. She needs no introduction to Muslims and is quite famous for all the wrong reasons elsewhere. She was the young wife of the Prophet (peace be upon him) and truly loved and honoured by him. She was a scholar and relator of so many Hadith (the recordings of what the Prophet said, did and approved of). Without her contribution to the Hadith collections we would have little understanding of the private life of the Prophet and miss key elements of how life in the Muslim home is supposed to be.

It's not just her scholarly attributes that make her a prime example for Muslim women the world over – she was also a very confident character. If she came across something she didn't know or understand she would find out about it and once she knew she would stand up for the truth. After the Prophet (peace be upon him) died she would often correct his companions. They would seek her rulings on matters. She was often asked to confirm important matters relating to what the Prophet (peace be upon him) had said or done. She was respected for her knowledge and tenacity for the truth.

An example was when they were fighting over whether the Prophet (peace be upon him) saw Allah on the night journey. Her response was that she was the first to question the Prophet (peace be upon him) on this matter, meaning that her opinion on the matter was the one to believe.

She had confidence, she wasn't shy to speak up, she wasn't concerned with what others thought of her – she was more concerned that the truth be preserved.

The lessons we take from this is that Muslim women play an important role as scholars in Islam and that their knowledge of the religion is to be respected and sought after, even by men. It highlights that we seek knowledge from the best source regardless of a person's gender.

One of the female companions was **Nusaibah bint Ka'b.** She was one of the two women at the second pledge of allegiance and a leader in her community. What stands out about her story is her participation in the battles of Uhud, Hunayn, Khaybar and the war of Yamamah. In fact, she was so skilful with her sword in the battle of Uhud that those who saw her were astonished. She played a key role in protecting the Prophet (peace be upon him) at the time when the Muslims fled the scene and ran towards the booty. She, along with her husband and two sons, fought to defend the Prophet (peace be upon him) to the extent that he said whichever direction he looked he saw her defending and protecting him.

She sustained thirteen major wounds, including a serious cut to her neck, and when the Prophet (peace be upon him) witnessed such bravery and courage, he made Du'a (supplication) for her and her children to have success in this life and for them to be with him in the Hereafter.

Another event that shows her strength of character was her ability to remain patient though the horrific death and mutilation of her son. She had the faith and understanding of their purpose in this life to see the blessing in his death.

Once, Nusaibah told the Prophet (peace be upon him) that the Qur'an only mentioned men. Then this verse was revealed:

Verily, the Muslims men and women, the believers men and women, the men and the women who are obedient (to Allah), the men and women who are truthful, the men and the women who are patient, the men and the women who are humble, the men and the women who give Sadaqat (i.e. Zakah and alms), the men and the women who observe fast, the men and the women who guard their chastity (from illegal sexual acts) and the men and the women who remember Allah much with their hearts and tongues, Allah has prepared for them forgiveness and a great reward (i.e. Paradise). – Qur'an 33:35

The lessons we can take away from her life are that women participated in key events including wars, were strong, courageous and active in the time of the Prophet (peace be upon him). She was never told to go home and that she shouldn't be involved in such matters. On the contrary, she was encouraged, praised and supplicated for.

Khadejah bint Khuwaylid was the first wife of the Prophet (peace be upon him). She was a very famous leader, a very wealthy woman, a very successful entrepreneur and businesswoman of the Quraish, fifteen years the senior of the Prophet (peace be upon him) and the one that gave birth to his children.

She was the one who the Prophet (peace be upon him) turned to after the first revelation. She was the one that took charge of that situation and took him to her cousin so he could understand what was going on. She was the first woman to embrace Islam. The example she is for us is how a woman can be a powerful and influential partner in marriage.

Here are some more examples of how Muslim women have shaped the world:

- **Al-Shifa bint Abduallah al Qurashiyah al-'Adawiyah** was literate at a time of illiteracy. She was involved in public administration and skilled in medicine. She used a preventative treatment against ant bites and the Prophet (peace be upon him) approved of her method and requested her to train other Muslim women (*Al-Shifa bint Abdullah* n.d.).

- **Rufaida Al-Aslamia** was an Islamic medical and social worker recognised as the first female nurse and surgeon in Islam. She lived at the time of the Prophet (peace be upon him) and nursed the wounded and dying in the battle of Badr. She was considered an expert healer (Yahya 2017).

- **Fatima al-Fihri** played a great role in the civilisation and culture in her community. She inherited a considerable amount of money from her father that she used to build a mosque and university for her community in 859, which was possibly the first university in the world. Students travelled from all over the world to study Islamic studies, astronomy, languages and sciences. Knowledge and use of the Arabic numbers in Europe came through this university (Kahn 2014).

- **Zubayda bint Ja'far al-Mansur** pioneered the ambitious project of digging wells and building service stations all along the pilgrimage route from Baghdad to Mecca. She was the wealthiest and most powerful woman in the world of her time. The famous Zubaida water spring in the outskirts of Mecca still carries her name (*Zubaidah bint Ja'far* n.d.).

- **Mariam al-Astrulabi** was a 10th century female astronomer in Aleppo, North Syria and was a maker of astrolabes, a branch of applied science of great status (*Extraordinary Women from the Golden Age of Muslim Civilisation* n.d.).

- **Sutayta Al-Mahāmali,** who lived in the second half of the 10th century, excelled in many fields such as Arabic literature, Hadith, and jurisprudence, as well as mathematics. It is said that she invented solutions to equations that have been cited by other mathematicians (*Extraordinary Women from the Golden Age of Muslim Civilisation* n.d.).

- **Labana of Cordoba** (Spain, ca. 10th century) was said to be well versed in the exact sciences, and could solve the most complex geometrical and algebraic problems known in her time. Her vast acquaintance with general literature obtained her the important employment of private secretary to the Umayyad Caliph of Islamic Spain, al-Hakam II (*[Then] Labana of Cordoba – Mathematician* 2012).

- **Arwa al-Sulayhi** was born in Haraz in 1048 AD in Yemen. She spent 70 years as the direct ruler of Yemen and lived to the age of 90. She built countless schools, mosques and even improved road infrastructure. She shifted the focus of the country from arms to agriculture and thus improved the economy. She also moved the capital from Sana to Jibla and turned her palace into a mosque (*Arwa al-Sulayhi* 2017).

- **Dhayfa Khatun** was the Queen of Aleppo for six years. During her six-year rule, she faced threats from Mongols, Seljuks, Crusaders and Khuarzmein. She was a popular queen because she removed injustices and unfair taxes throughout Aleppo. She favoured the poor and scientists and founded many charities to support them. In addition to her political and social roles, Dhayfa sponsored learning in Aleppo, where she founded two schools (Sadaf, M 2017).

- **Zaynab Al Shahda** (12th century) was a famous female calligrapher renowned for her work in Islamic law and Hadiths. She was highly praised and positioned. She was a brilliant, well-established teacher and many people had the opportunity to study with her and to receive their ijaza (permission to teach) from her. She spent her time studying science and literature (*Extraordinary Women from the Golden Age of Muslim Civilisation* n.d.).

- **Razia Sultana of Delhi, India** took power in Delhi for four years (1236-1240 CE). She was the only woman ever to sit on the throne of Delhi. Razia's ancestors were Muslims of Turkish descent who came to India in the 11th century. Contrary to custom, her father selected her, over her brothers, to be his successor. She established peace and order, encouraged trade, built roads, planted trees, dug wells, supported poets and painters and constructed schools and libraries (*Raiza Sultana* 2017).

- **Shajarat al-Durr** gained power in Cairo in 1250 CE. She brought the Muslims to victory during the Crusades and captured the King of France, Louis IX (*Shajar al-Durr* 2018).

- **Queen Amina of Zaria** (North Nigeria,16th century) was the first woman to become the queen in a male-dominated society. Amina is generally remembered for her fierce military exploits, her brilliant military strategy and, in particular, engineering and building great walled camps during her various campaigns. She is generally credited with the building of the famous Zaria wall (*Extraordinary Women from the Golden Age of Muslim Civilisation* n.d.).

- **Sameera Moussa** was an Egyptian nuclear physicist in the early 1900s who held a doctorate in atomic radiation and worked to make the medical use of nuclear technology affordable to all (Y, Dr. 2012).

- **Zaynab Al Ghazali,** born in 1917 in Egypt, is an example of persistence and true resilience. Her father encouraged her to be a leader in the community. By the age of eighteen she had founded an organisation for educating women and encouraging them to be active contributors to their community. She hosted lectures that attracted thousands of listeners. At the age of 50 she was imprisoned and tortured in the most horrendous ways and yet she still persisted in her work of helping women until she died (*Zainab al Ghazali* 2017).

These are just some of our role models of the past that show us that Muslim women have a significant role to play in public life, education, social reform, philanthropy and leadership. It is these women of Islam that show us how important our role is as Muslim women to lead the way for our own selves, our youth, our Ummah (Muslim community) and the global community. Their stories encourage us to step up to be our best selves. I know for me, as I rebuilt my life after leaving my first marriage, their stories of courage, confidence and resilience inspired me to keep going.

We are being watched closely. You only have to take note of the stares wherever we tread wearing our Islamic garments that identify us as the 'other'. We have an opportunity as Muslim women to make a significant difference and be the beacon of Islam just by stepping up and living with good intention and servitude to Allah alone.

May Allah give us all the strength and capability to be the best roles models of Islam!

Reflection Points:

1. How can we work better as an Ummah (Muslim community) to protect our new sisters in Islam from being taken advantage of while they are still learning about Islam?

2. Muslim women are barely mentioned in listings of influential Muslims, scientists, scholars and the like, or in books of the companions of the Prophet (peace be upon him). What can we do to help our girls have good role models in their life and education?

3. Where have you been holding back in your life and not stepping up in being the role model you can be in your family, neighbourhood and community?

To download a complimentary workbook and videos for this chapter go to www.stepupbonus.com

Chapter 2

Misconceptions, Misunderstandings or Misinformation?

'We cannot teach people anything; we can only help them discover it within themselves.' – Galileo Galilei

One of the strangest things that I have found since becoming a Muslim is how some people's attitude towards me have really changed. I haven't changed. I'm the same person. I still have the same brain and intelligence that I had before I became a Muslim, but somehow the whole concept of putting a scarf around my head seems to mean to people that I'm no longer intelligent. They talk down to me, like I don't understand English. Or perhaps I don't have an education. In fact, I've come across that a lot, where people have thought that Muslim women are uneducated. I find this really strange, given that most of my Muslim friends are more qualified than me. I only have a bachelor's degree and graduate diploma; they have master's degrees and PhDs. They are qualified doctors and engineers.

Interesting Fact:

The 2006 ABS Census shows that 17.5% of the Muslim Australian female population in the 18-plus age range has a qualification of bachelor's degree or higher. (This compares extremely favourably with the 18% of total Australian women in the same age range and with the same qualifications.) (McCue, H 2008)

There are a lot of myths out there about Muslim women and there are a lot of myths also within the Muslim world about Muslim women. I challenge the fact that it is just a misconception or a misunderstanding, I think there are times it is deliberate misinformation.

As I dug further into my research, I uncovered some really interesting facts and the more I looked the more I could see the subtleties that leave women 'less than' in the world, no matter her age, race, colour or creed.

- According to UN estimates, up to third of women alive today have experienced sexual or physical violence (*The World's Women 2015: Trends and Statistics* 2015)

- Although women make up 49.6% of the world's population, only 22.8% of parliamentarians are female worldwide (*Facts and figures: Leadership and political participation* 2017)

- In most countries, women only earn between 70% and 90% of men's wages – for the same work

- A woman is twice more likely to be illiterate than a man because she is twice as likely to miss out on education completely (*The World's Women 2015: Trends and Statistics* 2015)

There is further research by the Proceedings of the National Academy of Sciences of the United States of America that has indicated some very interesting facts about gender bias in the consideration of men and women for the same role within the sciences. Here are some of the conclusions from their research:

- 'Female' applicants were rated significantly lower than the 'males' in competence, whether they would be hired, and whether the scientist would be willing to mentor them.

- The scientists also offered lower starting salaries to the 'female' applicants: $26,507.94 compared to $30,238.10 for men.

- Both male and female scientists were equally guilty of committing the gender bias (Yurkiewicz, I 2012).

It is clear that the issue of misogyny stems from both men and women. The study discovered that the judgement of the female candidates was not coming from an intentional or conscious desire to hinder the progress of women, instead that these biases stemmed from implicit, unintentional, ingrained prejudices that had been internalised from repeated exposure to pervasive stereotypes that portray women as less competent than men.

The exposure is as subtle as what I discovered as I researched the Muslim women role models for Chapter 1 of this book. Firstly, I found that finding the women amongst the lengthy list of men was challenging. The books within my own bookshelf at home about the companions of the Prophet (peace be upon him) had only a small section at the back to cover the mention of the female companions. It was also interesting to note that they were always described based on who their father, brother, uncle or husband was. They didn't appear to have their own identity independent of the menfolk in their life. You will note that I chose to leave those details out of the descriptions of the Muslim women role models except in the cases where the male family member was a relevant part of the story.

The practical outcome of this subtle messaging makes it easy for women to internalise unfair criticisms as valid.

'I'm not good enough.'

'I don't deserve it.'

'I am not as good as a man.'

The more that we have internalised these messages the more we accept what is not acceptable and become complicit in the propagation of misogyny.

There is a global issue when it comes to women and how they are viewed. In our Islamic scriptures, we have the same issues coming through in how verses of the Qur'an and Hadith are interpreted. Without realising it we are internalising a message that women are less than men. In fact, Islam is not inherently a misogynistic religion. The message of Islam came to free women from the shackles of being 'owned' by men, buried alive at birth and treated as though they had a lower value.

Women in Islam retain their name after marriage, have the right to own their own business and have their own finances. They not only have a right to choose whom they marry, the marriage contract is not valid if she does not give her consent.

The Qur'an mentions women and men together, placing equal value, rights and responsibilities on each. Men and women are not treated the same because the nature and biology of men and women are different. These differences, however, do not make one superior over the other. These differences provide the opportunity to build stability within society as men and women complement each other, providing strength in one where the other has weakness.

So, if the Qur'an treats men and women as equals, why are we in a position of Islam being interpreted and practised in a misogynistic manner?

The answer lies within each one of us.

We cannot have a discussion about the interpretation of the verses of Qur'an or meanings of the Hadith without first looking within to see what we are bringing to the discussion from our own selves. While the Nafs (our ego) is directly involved, the conversation is tainted by our own desires, emotional connections to past experiences and injustices.

It is when we find our neutral state, detach from the Dunyah (this worldly life) and can be present in the moment that we can then come from a place of egoless understanding and find the true balance Allah intended for men and women.

I am not a scholar of Fiqh (Islamic jurisprudence) and will not get into Fiqhi (jurisprudential) discussion here. My goal with this book is to help every reader find their true neutral, egoless, peaceful and thoughtful self so we can all be part of the solution rather than perpetuating the myths and misconceptions about Muslim women in Islam. Whether we are conscious of it or not, we all have a role to play in it.

Here is an example of how we, as women, are contributing to the message that women are 'less than' men. I see it show up in the entrepreneurial space all the time. A Muslim man can sell an inferior product or service at a premium price and our sisters in Islam will pay them, yet when offered something of higher quality and of more value to them by a Muslim woman, they value it less and struggle to commit. Often they will barter for a reduced investment when what is being offered is already being undervalued at the asking price.

As women we are subconsciously devaluing other women and ourselves. By not pricing our work at market value and by discounting our pricing we are devaluing our work. As women when we ask another woman to reduce her pricing, we are devaluing her. We do it all the time without thinking. It is the 'without thinking' part that is the problem. It is deeply ingrained female oppression that we are living throughout our lives.

Education is key in this solution. We need to educate ourselves so we understand the nature of the human psyche in order to master our own Nafs (ego) and seek to live within the limits set by Allah without transgressing the rights of others, and live at a higher level of consciousness so we are part of the solution and not perpetuating the problem.

We need to educate the next generation to be strong, resilient men and women who will do a better job of building respectful cohesion between both genders.

Muslim women play a key role in bringing balance to our Ummah. We are most often the first source of education for our children. By being conscious of the messages we are teaching our children through our behaviour, words and responses to others, we can point our children in the right direction to equality and leadership within the Ummah, regardless of their gender.

I think one of the beautiful stories that show how the Prophet (peace be upon him) treated women in terms of their ability and their intelligence was on the occasion when the Muslims were denied access to perform Hajj (pilgrimage) in Mecca, as a condition for the peace treaty. The Prophet (peace be upon him) accepted that condition, but the Muslims were really upset and refused to leave.

It was a very difficult matter for the Prophet and so he consulted his wife Umm Salamah about it and asked her what was the best course of action. Here is how the story goes:

After the Prophet (peace be upon him) signed the peace treaty with the disbelievers of Quraish, he then commanded his companions to slaughter their animals and shave their heads, thus completing the rituals of *Umrah* at the valley of Hudaibiyyah. As a condition of the treaty they had to return to Madinah without entering Makkah. The companions were so saddened that they would not be allowed to perform the *Umrah*, which they had set out to do, and not a single one of them got up to carry out the Prophet's (peace be upon him) order. After repeating this command three times, still no one got up to perform his orders. The Prophet (peace be upon him) went and entered upon his wife, Umm Salamah, and he told her what had happened. Upon hearing his complaint, she told him to go out and not talk to any of them until he slaughtered his animal and shaved his head. The Prophet (peace be upon him) took her advice and acted upon it promptly. When the companions saw the Prophet (peace be upon him) slaughter his animal and shave his head, they all followed him in doing so.

The Prophet (peace be upon him) sought his wives' advice around matters relating to his community, his state and his leadership. It is an important precedent for us because it demonstrates the value that he placed on women being an integral part of society.

Women even have the right to correct the Muslim leadership and the leadership has to be humble enough to accept it.

There is the story of the woman of the Quraish tribe who used the Qur'an to argue publicly with 'Umar (the caliph or ruler of the time) only a few years after the death of the Prophet (peace be upon him). 'Umar wanted to cap the value of the dowry, a gift that must be given to a woman for her personal use. The woman criticised his plan using Qur'anic verses to justify her disagreement, and upon hearing her argument 'Umar rescinded, saying, 'The woman is right and 'Umar is wrong.'

We have also already learnt about Aisha Bint Abu Bakr and her confidence in correcting the companions.

As women, we have the opportunity to be leaders and in this era, when we are in the spotlight, we are the ones that stand out in our Ummah. I see that we have a responsibility to be leaders. I'm not suggesting that each and every one of you has to go out and take on roles of leadership in the greater global community. What I am talking about is leadership just in the way we live our daily life. If you are taking charge of your daily life, if you're behaving as somebody who is confident, resilient and patient, showing all the great attributes that Allah wishes from us, and you're out there representing the Muslim world, then insha Allah (Allah willing), bit by bit, people are going to realise that the fabric of the Muslim woman and of Islam is quite different to the rhetoric they've been hearing in the media.

It will also play an effect within our Ummah (community) as well. When women work together with the brothers in order to lead our community, we have a very holistic approach to unity, to compassion and to an Ummah that will succeed moving forward, insha Allah (Allah willing).

Muslim women across the globe are doing incredible things. They are creative, passionate and have tenacity despite the barriers that are before them. This is why it is so important that as a Muslim Ummah (community) we support them to succeed in their ventures, because every time one of them crosses the path of a non-Muslim they challenge any misconceptions or stereotypes that person may have.

Let's be a part of the solution rather than innocently continuing the problem!

Reflection Points:

1. What ways can you see women participating in the decisions of your local community?

2. Next time you are talking to your children, grandchildren, nieces, nephews or younger siblings notice if there is any gender bias in the language you use. (For example, do you expect different behaviours, manners or results from boys and girls?)

3. Which is the one area in your life you would like to take charge of and show more leadership

To download a complimentary workbook and videos for this chapter go to www.stepupbonus.com

Chapter 3

Where Is My Knight In Shining Armour?

'Our greatest glory is not in never falling, but in rising every time we fall.' – Confucius, philosopher

Emotionally, physically and spiritually empty. I walked away from my first marriage like a zombie and began a journey, step by step, of coming back to life.

Those little faces, my three young children, were the motivation to really push myself to get better.

Hours of pleading with Allah for the answers led to me moving to a completely different town. I decided to live near my father so I had family support to regain my health. My breathing had become so laboured and I was having many attacks in the night where I struggled to get even a bit of air into my lungs. I was on the maximum medication they were able to prescribe me and nothing was working. My father, who also suffers from asthma, had not had to use his puffer where he lives, so moving to live near him was the perfect solution.

I went to my husband at the time and suggested I move away for three months to get well. I truly believed as I asked that this was going to be a temporary solution and, reluctantly, he agreed. I was so surprised, but then why should I be surprised when I asked Allah for help? When we ask for the solutions from Allah, He gives us the most beautiful solutions. This is the first step, in any moment in our life when we're ready to step up, when you truly put your intention for the sake of Allah and you ask Allah for His guidance, the doors open in ways you never imagined.

And whosoever fears Allah and keeps his duty to Him, He will make a way for him to get out (from every difficulty). And He will provide him from (sources) he never could imagine. – Qur'an 65:2-3

Instructions from my doctor were to see someone to take over my medical care as soon as I arrived. Standing in the waiting room, I was reading the notice board and I noticed that there was a playgroup right near the place that I was living. I decided that might be a good way of settling into my new environment and finding some good company with other mothers with similarly aged children.

The doctor I saw helped me into a program with a psychologist for weekly sessions at no cost. The following week, I went to the playgroup and discovered that this playgroup was particularly for people who had come out of or were still struggling with domestic violence. Their ten-week program to help women understand and escape domestic violence was just about to begin.

Every single door was opening for me to move forward. All it took was for me to take the first step!

Indeed, Allah will not change the condition of a people until they change what is in themselves. – Qur'an 13:11

I stepped up and changed the condition within myself.

It is our responsibility to look after ourselves physically, emotionally and spiritually. It may well be that all three are suffering. When I left I started caring for myself again. I regularly saw the doctor, I saw the psychologist, I read every book she told me to, I showed up at every class on domestic violence, I walked daily for exercise, I ate well and I started attending online Islamic classes.

36

I was filling up my very empty cup, spiritually, emotionally and physically.

We often have excuses as to why we can't do this. I was on my own with three young children, very little income and far from any mosque or Islamic centre. When I first moved to my father's town, I was the only Muslim with Hijab to be seen. As they say, '*Where there's a will, there's a way*'.

If you're not well and lacking energy, seek help.

If you're finding it really hard to concentrate in your prayer and connect with Allah, seek help.

If you're struggling in your relationships, seek help.

If you're finding yourself depressed, angry or generally unhappy, seek help.

Seek help from the people who are going to help you out of your situation, who have the knowledge, experience and good character to support you well.

I had a dear friend that I made through attending her classes at the mosque before I left who was a key player in helping me see the light around my situation. Yes, my doctor's words were the ones that stunned me into action, but she played a very pivotal role in helping me understand Islam better and realising that nothing I was experiencing was a part of the religion and that I did not have to put up with it.

May Allah reward her for that.

The first step in being a leader is being the leader of your own self!

Waiting for a knight in shining armour to come is wasting precious time. Not only is being rescued unlikely, it isn't even helpful. Leading our self to a better life is more powerful and sustainable. We have the opportunity to grow. We are less likely to fall back into misery.

Here are some tips on how you can start being the leader in your own life:

- **Stop Over-Thinking.** Allow life to unfold as a beautiful mystery. Allah is The Controller over all our affairs so we don't need to be in control. As we allow the future to be where it belongs, as something not yet in existence, and we put the past away, done and dusted, we are left with so much less to think about. Alhamdu Lillah (praise be to Allah).

- **Accept What Is.** Stop pushing. Everything will happen according to Allah's plan. Our job is to do the best we can with this present moment. Yes, sometimes we will have feelings about the way things are – that is natural. Remember in those moments that this life is a test. Not all the answers are going to come easy.

- **Be Still**. Breathe slowly and deeply and take in what is around you. Have you noticed the little things, the details, lately? How are you feeling? What's on your mind?

- **Stop Comparing Yourself to Others.** Allah has told us He has given to some and not to others, not as a preference over them but as a test. We can be tested with patience by what we do not have, and by following the advice of the Prophet (peace be upon him) looking to those who have less than us provides us with opportunity to be grateful. We are also tested with gratitude for what we are blessed with. Do we become complacent? Do we use it for good or for evil? Your tests are your own, tailored by Allah, just for you.

- **Take Actions that Scare You.** Or, in other words, face your fears and do it anyway. We don't grow living in our comfort zone. It's outside that zone that we find the brilliance and beauty of this life. That's where we discover what we are truly capable of.

- **Cherish Your Friends.** You are as your friends are, the advice the Prophet (peace be upon him) gave us. When you are with beloved friends who inspire you to do good work together, time flies, life is full and worries seem far away.

- **Know Your Strengths**. We are so good at picking out our weak-nesses, our failings – all the things we could do better. Stop and notice what you have achieved, how much you improved, what you do well. In there lies the answer to your purpose. We each have gifts of strength that Allah has blessed us with. Seek them out and see what good you can do with them.

- **Eat well.** Instant gratification on chocolate, sweets, coffee and chips does not compare to the energy you have when your body is fuelled well. As they say, you are what you eat. If we eat junk we become … not something I aspire to.

- **Speak To Yourself Kindly**. We are usually our own worst enemy. Interestingly, the way we treat ourselves is how we allow others to treat us. Next time you are wondering why people don't treat you well, look inward and see how you are speaking to yourself!

- **Exercise Regularly.** A daily walk to brush away the cobwebs, lower the cortisol and breathe the fresh air. Cortisol is the hormone that is activated when we are under stress. We live in a very busy time where stress levels are high and as a result we often have this hor-mone running amuck in our system causing many different medical conditions.

- **Don't Let People Walk All Over You.** Say no! It's such a small word yet so hard to say. The day I was able to say no was one of the turning points of my life. And guess what? The people I care about are still hanging around – they didn't run away!

- **Forgive Yourself.** Forgive others. Forgiveness sets us free. It isn't about the other person at all – most of the time they are oblivious to the hurt that you hold onto. When you forgive them, you let go of the hurt you are carrying and are free from its effects. Forgiving our-selves is even more powerful – holding ourselves trapped in our past failings is paralysing and limits our personal growth.

- **Stay Away from Negative People.** And if you can't stay away, minimise their impact on you! Seek out those whose company is like having your battery charged, you walk away feeling like you could conquer the world.

- **Don't Be a Negative Person.** There is always hope. Allah assures us of this over and over in the Qur'an when He tells us that He won't burden us with more than we can bear and when He tells us that with difficulty comes ease. If we remain stuck in negativity it is similar to denying this truth from Allah.

- **Allow Yourself to Feel Whatever You're Feeling.** Feelings come from our thought in that moment. From one moment to the next we can move through the experience of different feelings, which follow what is going on in our mind. The more we allow ourselves to be present in the moment and feel, the smoother the feelings move on, just like clouds passing in the sky.

- **Embrace Your Imperfections**. We were created with them as a blessing. A blessing so that we have reason to turn back to Allah when we get it wrong. Love your nose, your body, your voice, your hair, your messy writing, your clumsiness. Whatever your imperfections are, they are a part of who you are and what makes you unique, special and beautiful.

- **Expand Your Mind.** Read! What was the first word revealed of the Qur'an? ... Read! We could study our entire life, every single day and never run out of things to learn. You never know, you might find your purpose and passion in this life.

- **Unplug.** From technology, from people, from routine, from the hustle and bustle. The dishes, laundry, vacuuming, cooking, children, parents, spouse will still all be there waiting for you when you plug back in, it just won't seem as overwhelming as it did before.

- **Be of Service**. With pure intention for the sake of Allah, and actions to be of service to Him and Him alone, you will find your true purpose. Remember even a smile is a charity. You never know what a difference one smile may have made to someone's day!

- **Just Be You.** You are perfect just the way you are! You are exactly as Allah created you to be.

Take that first step and Allah will open all the doors you need moving forward. Insha Allah (Allah willing).

Reflection Points:

1. Who are the people in your life who are supportive, the ones you can reach out to when you need help?

2. What one thing are you going to do today to start taking charge of your life?

3. One of the barriers to taking charge in your life is your inner self-talk. To help you with this I have put together a free master class for you called 'Banish Toxic Self Talk' and you can access it here: www.banishtoxicselftalk.com

To download a complimentary workbook and videos for this chapter go to www.stepupbonus.com

Chapter 4

What Does My Childhood Have To Do With It?

> *'Our eyes are the windows to the soul, and only when our eyes are free from yesterday's scratches will we see today with clarity.'* – *Sydney Banks*

I was thirteen when somewhere deep inside of me came the strength to tell him to never come into my room again.

It was a defining moment.

I had become stronger psychologically than the man who had been abusing me week after week for months. Finally, my bedroom became my sanctuary. I was safe in there and I achieved that myself.

I had been desperately hoping that someone would rescue me, someone would figure it out, and someone would come along and put a stop to what was happening. In the end, I was strong enough on my own.

I learnt a lesson in that moment when he listened and didn't return to my room. That lesson was: **Don't rely on others; do it yourself**.

That lesson remained with me. I even battle with it sometimes now. Do it myself means, 'Don't trust anyone else to do it', 'Don't rely on anyone else to do it' and the hardest one of all, 'Don't ask for help; do it yourself'.

Living with these internal messages as an adult I became a drained, over-whelmed and a worn-out person. All self-created by my belief that I had to do everything myself.

Many of the experiences we have as a child pre-frame the way we deal with things as adults. Our immature interpretation of events can remain as stuck and rigid thinking about people, situations and about ourselves. We can be quite unaware that they are there and believe that the way we are feeling and reacting as adults is coming from the current situation we are in.

Some of the common self-beliefs that I found in myself and see in the women that I coach are:

- I'm not good enough

- I don't deserve it

- I am not important

- I am not worthy

- It's my fault

- My opinion isn't important

When we have these thoughts going on beneath the surface it can influence our lives in so many ways. Things we find challenging but can't put our finger on why.

For example:

- As an entrepreneur, not believing we are worthy or good enough can make sales calls, especially the part where we discuss money, very difficult and often unsuccessful.

- As a mother, not believing we are important often means we put ourselves last, most often believing it is the noble thing to do, to then find ourselves yelling at the children, or becoming quite ill.

- As a wife, thinking our opinion isn't important can lead to very self-destructive behaviour, not speaking up when something is not good for us, allowing things to happen to us that are not OK and then quietly suffering expecting that one day someone will realise and make it all better.

- I don't deserve it can mean we don't put ourselves forward for the promotion at work or ask for what we need from family and friends.

All of these examples are innocently self-inflicted and self-destructive. I say innocently because for the most part we remain unaware that this is what is happening.

For the entrepreneur, it may look to her like her niche is tight-fisted and won't spend on her product or services. She will be oblivious to the fact that at the point when she starts to talk about money her insecurities around not being good enough have kicked in and the potential customer has sensed a disconnection in their interaction and loses the trust that had been developing between them.

The mother who is losing it at her children and feeling ill innocently be-lieves that if her children just behaved better and listened to her more then she would be OK. She feels resentful that she has to do everything and that no one sees how hard she is working and helps her out.

The wife that is being treated unkindly feels scared to stand up for her rights. She worries that if she dares mention her opinion on the matter that she will be blamed and harmed for speaking up.

The woman who has worked hard at the company, given 100%, has the qualifications and experience to do the job, holds back from asking for the promotion because she believes someone else in the company deserves it more than her. She secretly hopes that they will ask her, but holds back and tries hard not to look like she is keen in case they don't choose her because she doesn't want to look foolish that she even thought she had a chance.

So much of what we are experiencing in our adult life that we are struggling with stems back to the experience that we had or the constant messages that we took from what's happened and what's been said to us as children.

The way it plays out in our adult life is very subconscious. We are not necessarily consciously aware that these things are going on. We just notice that we find it really hard in certain circumstances.

What is happening is that we have stuck or rigid thinking that takes over in these situations. We are unable to experience each situation with new possibility; instead, we revisit the same thinking we have always had.

If we track back through my history it is easy to see where the pattern of accepting abusive behaviour stemmed from. From very early on I took on the role of everything being my fault. It was my fault that there was a lot of stress around my existence: my parents were still completing their medical degrees and were not anticipating having a family so soon. There was tension in the house and then my parents divorced. I did what many children do: I thought it was my fault.

My first experience of being bullied was in year four. Three boys from my class would take me hostage at recess and lunch, give me a branch to use as a broom and tell me to sweep the floor of their pretend house. When I would escape to join my friends, they would capture me again and dig their nails into my wrists drawing blood to show me it wasn't OK for me to escape. I had a male teacher and I went to him to complain about how I was being treated, only to be told that boys are like that. He did nothing. I was left to put up with being captured at lunch and recess until they got bored of their game.

My first year of high school was the clincher. There was the sexual abuse that went on for about 18 months, my grandmother dying, my aunt moving away, my father in another state and school was a mess!

I sprained my ankle three times, and injured my finger that year. The girls in my netball team bullied me for being accident-prone and for being a 'square' for having good grades. They rolled my pencils down the school driveway, tied my gym shoes to the school rafters and kneed me from behind as we would get off the school bus. Worse still, I was growing so fast that my school pants were always above my ankles leading to another reason to tease me. This constant bullying from girls two years older than me left me feeling as though I didn't belong – something that was reinforced as I moved into the maths and physics stream in my final years of school and was one of only two girls in the class.

So, I took all this on board and believed that perhaps I didn't deserve to be treated well, perhaps I didn't deserve to have a good life.

So when an abusive person walked into my life, I believed him when he blamed me, because I was good at accepting the blame. I believed him when he told me I didn't deserve him, because that was what I believed about myself. I accepted the unacceptable because I didn't believe I deserved better.

I became accustomed to living in it. I didn't like it, I was unhappy. In fact, I was becoming incredibly ill as a result of the stress from the abuse.

But I knew how to navigate that and my whole life and every ounce of my energy and being was taken up in navigating through that maze of how to make sure we didn't have another episode of abuse. *Walking on eggshells.*

To me, the alternative looked like this: leave and be hunted down and killed, or I would be forever fighting with him over my children and my children would be put in a more difficult situation; we would never be free of all of this.

46

Fear of how it might turn out made it appear easier to stay, until the day my doctor asked who would look after my children if I died. That then became a scarier option. If I die there is no one there to protect my children.

My thinking was not logical. It was influenced by deep subconscious thought patterns that made it appear as if there were no choices.

There are always choices!

Of course, I look back now in retrospect and realise I should have left years earlier.

I know that is a pretty extreme example, but sometimes it takes a really extreme example for us to understand what I am talking about. The reality is that every single one of us has a leader within us; every single one of us is capable of navigating this life in a very strong and powerful way. But when we get messed up in the way we are thinking about it, we can be paralysed in a situation that is totally unhealthy for us, emotionally, spiritually and physically.

I am truly blessed, because every single step of the way when I was not sure of the direction, I would ask Allah and Allah would bring the right people in my life to help me, every single time. I have been incredibly blessed with those who I needed to support me emotionally, with those who I needed to support me spiritually, and with those who I needed to support me physically.

All came from Allah, all came from trusting in him. But the point of this chapter is for us to understand how the programming of our childhood is playing out in our adulthood and that it might be leaving us stuck and unable to be able see the way forward.

In those cases the answer is with Allah, as He knows best. Do as I did and cry into your prayer mat and ask for His help, then start making steps forward. One foot in front of the other!

STEP UP — EMBRACE THE LEADER WITHIN

Reflection Points:

1. Can you see where you have picked up some ideas from experiences in your past and held onto them and now they are holding you back?

2. Are there any parts of your life where you feel stuck, feel like you are going around in the same circle over and over? Is it possible to think about that differently, now that you know it is likely some stuck, old thinking that is holding you there?

3. Make a choice today to lead your life, rather than let old thinking lead you! Imagine what that would look like ...

To download a complimentary workbook and videos for this chapter go to www.stepupbonus.com

Chapter 5

Who's The Boss?

'Shall I call the police?'

I heard her voice from across the road. I looked up and I could see faces in the windows of my neighbours. I was standing in my driveway, between my two boys, both 6'4", one hand on each of their chests, with them both very angry, yelling at each other. In that moment I really had no care in the world what my neighbours thought. My attention, my concentration, was 100% on my boys.

They had been through so much over the years, through the violence of the first marriage, through the confusion of six years of being tugged one way or another by the family court system. And they were angry. Often it came out at each other.

This episode, however, was the first time we'd had something like this in a very long time.

And the difference this time was I was in charge.

I was calm.

It didn't feel out of control. I was not scared. I knew exactly what to do. I would look at one in the eye and say, 'No, you're not going to hurt your brother'. I would turn to the other and say, 'You're going to go for a walk and cool down'.

I would turn back to the other one again and say, 'No, you'll not hurt your brother'. It took a while. Eventually, my eldest did walk and it gave me the opportunity to be with my second son and help him cool down.

That is leadership as a parent.

But it's one of the hardest things for many of us to do. And it took me a very, very long time to reach the point where I was able to do that. In fact, back in 2011, I actually thought it was completely hopeless. That I was never going to be able to help my boys at all. All the professionals that we had worked with had said it was too late, that since they had reached their teens or almost teens, that at this stage, if they weren't showing signs of change, we would most likely have to wait until they were adults.

You know how depressing that is for a parent to hear that about their child?

I was determined not to give up and, Alhamdu Lillah (praise be to Allah), I was blessed with an opportunity to learn about parenting from a very different perspective.

I was invited to come along to a parenting course that was running at my daughter's children's centre. I'd done so many parenting courses and read so many books, I really wasn't that interested, but they asked if I would come along because they had a group of Muslim women attending and they wanted to make sure that they managed things well culturally. I came along to help with that and be the cultural translator, I suppose.

After the first class my mind was blown away by how amazing it was. This was something so completely different and I could see how it could be the answer, not just to helping my children heal from all they went through, but also myself as well.

I had been studying my Graduate Diploma of Teaching and Learning, but after having learnt this way of parenting, I had to become certified to teach other parents how to parent this way, too. I gave up on being a classroom teacher to become a Peaceful Parenting Coach. That is where the Peaceful Parenting Academy began.

In the previous chapter, we talked about what our childhood has got to do with it. Being a parent is the best opportunity to discover all the interesting things that we have decided about ourselves as children and have hung onto as adults, because children have a knack of bringing it out in us. Every single time we feel ourselves overwhelmed by an emotional reaction that seems to have come out of the blue – because our children did or said something or they're behaving in a particular way – it's a reminder, a very subconscious reminder, of something from the past.

They say it is children pushing our buttons, but I know differently now. In fact, our children don't push our buttons, our children are amazingly beautiful, intelligent beings that need our connection to feel well, to behave as their best self. When they feel disconnected from that, lose that connection with us, then their behaviour goes off-track.

One of the first places to look when you see your child off-track is at your own self, because 90% of the time the reason for our children's off-track behaviour is the fact that we ourselves are off-track. We ourselves have something going on that is keeping us from being truly present in the moment and connected. It is a brilliant way of parenting and a wonderful way of understanding how things work, because it simplifies everything.

Either our children are on-track or off-track.

When they are on-track they are intelligent and their intelligence is operating at its full potential, both emotionally and intellectually. They are able to learn, think well, they have empathy for others and they are creative.

When they are off-track or feeling disconnected, then you will find that stubbornness showing, that rigidity in their thinking, their inability to reason. It is often what we call manipulative or stubborn behaviour, but the reality is that it is not that at all. In fact, many a child has been labelled as being stubborn or shy or manipulative or aggressive or any other of these labels that we give children, because they have persistent behaviour of a particular kind and the reality is that it is just a symptom of them being off-track. All they are looking for is that good, healthy connection that will bring their little minds back on track.

Seeing how this all worked has given me a way forward with my family, with my children and with my own self.

In fact, it has given me the opportunity to be the leader in my family.

Not many people understand that that is what I am doing though. It is misunderstood quite a lot because peaceful parenting is misunderstood. There is a misconception out there that parenting has to be about rewards and consequences and that if I am not doing rewards and consequences then I am not leading and parenting my children. Rewards and consequences, as every parent knows, don't work. They may sometimes, but a lot of the time we either run out of consequences, or the rewards don't work.

The reason why is because the behaviour isn't about the children thinking, 'I am going to do something bad', it is because they are not thinking at all, because they are emotionally off-track. And so, they're not thinking to themselves, 'I better not do that, otherwise I'll miss out on the rewards', or, 'I better behave myself so I don't get that consequence'. They are just not thinking. When we understand that, we can approach our children in a much better way, in a connecting and respectful way that follows the Sunnah of the Prophet (peace be upon him).

By the way, this doesn't mean we don't set limits with the children – of course we do! If we want to achieve limit setting with children, we have to first look at ourselves, because 90% of the success of setting limits, of being a leader with our children, is parenting from a peaceful place inside. When you obtain that peaceful place inside you step up as a leader and then the other 10% is a few awesome tools that I am happy to teach you in the Peaceful Parenting Academy.

Being a leader in our family means building awesome relationships and connections with our children which then become the super protective factor, becomes the protective factor of our children going off-track and experimenting with alcohol, with drugs, with sex and other things that all Muslim parents fear will happen once their children are in their teens.

It starts with us and when we step up as a true leader, as a parent, our children are more willing to follow. They are always going to resist some-times. There is always going to be the times when it doesn't work out, but the thing is it's not about building perfect families and it's not about everyone being perfect. It's about knowing what to do in that moment, taking charge and being a leader in that moment.

There are some really important Islamic reasons why we need to step up as leaders in our parenting as well.

We have been taught:

The Messenger of Allah, peace be upon him, said, 'Every one of you is a shepherd and is responsible for his flock. The leader of people is a guardian and is responsible for his subjects. A man is the guardian of his family and he is responsible for them. A woman is the guardian of her husband's home and his children and she is responsible for them. The servant of a man is a guardian of the property of his master and he is responsible for it. No doubt, every one of you is a shepherd and is responsible for his flock'. – Sahih Muslim and Sahih Bukhari

I witness a lot of parents taking this responsibility seriously when it comes to their children's education, housing, clothing and entertainment, but I see a lacking of attention when it comes to the emotional development and wellbeing of our children. We are focused on the intellectual develop-ment of our children but not our children's emotional intelligence. For our children to grow into resilient, articulate and strong leaders, they need healthy family connections to lead them to strong emotional wellbeing.

Let's explore how the Qur'an guides us in parenting:

By an act of mercy from Allah, you [Prophet] were gentle in your dealings with them – had you been harsh, or hard-hearted, they would have dispersed and left you – so pardon them and ask forgiveness for them. Consult with them about matters, then, when you have decided on a course of action, put your trust in Allah: Allah loves those who put their trust in Him. If Allah helps you [believers], no one can overcome you; if He forsakes you, who else can help you? Believers should put their trust in Allah'. – Qur'an 3:159

Now this verse from the Qur'an isn't specifically about parenting, but what we are going to do is actually take the meaning of it and apply it in a parenting setting to see how it is actually teaching us something that is very helpful in regards to how we deal with our children.

The first part – **By an act of mercy from Allah, you [Prophet] were gentle in your dealings with them**.

While Allah is talking about the way the Prophet (peace be upon him) dealt with people in general, let's look at it from a parenting perspective because our children are little people. They are little human beings and they deserve as much, maybe even more, kindness and respect than a general person in our life does.

The next part of the verse is, **'had you been harsh, or hard-hearted, they would have dispersed and left you.**

That means uttering harsh words, having a harsh-heart – you know, dealing with people in an unkind manner. Now, what Allah is telling us here is had the Prophet (peace be upon him) spoken to people in a harsh way, if he'd been really hard in the manner in which he had called people into Islam, they would have scattered, they would not have been attracted to him, they would not have come to him, they would have run.

Now, let's put that into a parenting context, shall we? If we are treating our children harshly and if we are being hard-hearted towards our children, then surely they are going to scatter, too. Instead of being drawn to

54

us, instead of being connected with us, they are going to find someone else to be connected to. Islam is going to seem hard to them, family life is going to seem hard to them, so they are going to seek out where they feel comfortable, where they feel at home – somewhere else – and we don't want that, do we?

The warning here is entirely relevant to us as parents, too. If we are severe and harsh-hearted to our children we are going to push them away.

Ask yourself these questions to see if you are being harsh:

- When your child makes a mistake, do you get mad at them, do you treat them harder than you would treat someone else who made that mistake?

- Are you getting angry over the small things?

- Are you ignoring them when they need you because you feel overwhelmed?

- Do you find yourself resorting to raising your voice and/or hitting the children to get them to do what you want them to?

Which brings us to the next bit of the verse – **So pardon them and ask forgiveness for them.**

Now, how many times do our children make mistakes? Pretty much all the time, don't they? Children are little people and they are going to make mistakes and they are going to make even more mistakes than adults make because they are still learning about life and they are not fully developed mentally. There is a lot of change going on for them, there is a lot to learn, and yet when they make a mistake, how hard are we on them? Are we really being forgiving towards them?

Instead of being harsh with them, are we stopping and making Dua' to Allah? 'Allah guide my child to the best way. Oh, Allah, my child made this mistake, forgive my child and guide my child to the straight path.'

Are we doing that or are we getting really angry and upset and frustrated and blaming our child and getting cross with them and saying things like:

'You're driving me crazy.'

'You make me so mad!'

'I have told you a hundred times.'

'Why can't you get it right?'

'How many times do I have to tell you?'

Remember our last chapter in this book: what messages are our children learning from our language when we speak to them this way?

The reality is actually our own feelings are our own responsibility and our child is not driving us crazy and they are not making us mad because that is actually not possible. Our feelings are coming from our own frustrated thinking.

We are having our own mad feelings and we are having our own crazy feelings from what we are thinking and what is going on with us, and then we are not able to be forgiving and loving towards our child.

Now, if it was a stranger who did the same thing and they came to us and said, 'Ugh, look I've really stuffed up, I did … ', would we be harsh with them? No, we would be forgiving. We would say, 'You know, Allah can forgive anything except associating partners with Him. So seek forgiveness for what you've done and Allah will forgive you, insha Allah'.

Why not treat our children the same way – teaching them about repentance and forgiveness as we lovingly support them through their mistakes, helping them to develop their problem-solving skills?

Instead, we are treating them like it is the end of the world that they have done something wrong. And then our heart becomes hard towards them and we find it hard to be loving towards them, and then they feel rejected and they feel that our love for them is dependent upon their behaviour. That is the worst possible thing we can do to a child, to make them believe that they have to behave a particular way in order for us to be OK and love them.

Our feelings and our reactions are our responsibility, not our children's, and our love for them should be unconditional regardless of their behaviour. When they stuff up they need our love even more. The child that is struggling and making lots of mistakes is a child struggling with something in life, they do not need more harshness and more hardness from us – they need more love. They need more connection, they need us to be there for them, for us to be the rock for them and the one to show them the light and which direction to go.

When Allah says, **'So pardon them and ask forgiveness for them'**, this applies to us with our children as well.

The next bit I know a lot of parents struggle with – **Consult with them about matters.**

A lot of us think that parenting is about controlling our children and it is about having control of everything, and society places this pressure on us as well. Society says, 'Control your children', and if your children aren't behaving you are often rebuked with, 'Why aren't you controlling your children?' It puts a lot of pressure on parents. In turn, the parents put that pressure on their children.

In reality, we don't have control over our children and trying to have control over our children is not the answer. Allah is the only one who has control over anything, and the only control we have over anyone is ourselves and even that is not 100% because Allah has the final control over us.

Control is not the answer.

We are not here to control our children; we are here to invite them to a good life and to lead the way by example by being their ally through everything.

To consult them in their affairs is when you allow children to have their say, when you show them that you respect their opinion and that you are going to listen to them. That doesn't mean that you have to do it their way. What you are showing them is that they are somebody who is important in the running of the family, that they are an important part of the family. You are also teaching them to have some responsibility and some thought about how things happen. And it may well be that, when you consult them, the idea that they come up with is completely ridiculous and not something that you can implement. In that case, we don't put them down, instead, we thank them for their input and we use words like, 'You know what? I can see where you're coming from with that thought and it's a really good thought. In this particular case, I'm not sure we can do it that way, how about … ', and then you start adding your ideas to it, but you have acknowledged and shown respect and really shown your child that you listened to them. You have shown them that they're an important member of the family.

The next part is: **Then, when you have decided on a course of action, put your trust in Allah.**

There is a Sahih Hadith from the Abu Dawud, Tirmithi and Ibn Majah collection where the Prophet (peace be upon him) said, 'Al-mustashār mu'taman', which means 'One who is consulted for advice is trustworthy'. I like that Hadith because it supports the idea that if you seek advice from someone then it builds that trust and they feel trusted. So just imagine the effect on our children if we sought their advice and showed them that we value their opinion.

When somebody feels trusted, they actually don't want to lose that and they are more likely to act upon that trust by being more trustworthy. So, instead of doubting our children and not trusting them, if we entrust them, then we are actually building that trust and building that feeling that they are trusted, and as a result they are actually more likely to be trustworthy.

> *'Leaders don't create followers, they create more leaders.' –*
> *Ralph Nader, attorney*

Sometimes we are actually making it harder on ourselves because we think we have to control and we have to manage things so that our children don't get into trouble, whereas if we build safe and trusting relationships with them then they are more likely to act on that in a trustworthy and safe manner.

Then when you have taken a decision, put your trust in Allah. I love this reminder, because every time I am not putting my trust in Allah, I am panicking about my children. When I put my trust in Allah, I don't panic and I am in a calm place and I am in the best place to be the best parent for my children. We forget that we are not in control of the outcome. Our job is to do our best at parenting our children in the best way possible. Whether this means they become the devout, pious Muslims that we hope for is out of our hands. This is already written by Allah. When we let go of the outcome, we find peace and solace in trusting Allah.

The other point we take from this part of the verse is that once the family has been consulted and a decision made, it is better for us to stick with that decision and put our trust in Allah. If we are firm on the fact that that's the right thing to do, then stick with it. When we waver in our decision, then our children are going to doubt our authority, they are going to sense our indecision and find it confusing.

I actually think that running a family is like steering a ship and we are trying to steer a ship through troubled water, we are trying to avoid the icebergs, and the reefs and steer our ship through stormy weather. We need to be the captain of the ship, and so once we have made a decision to steer the ship in a particular direction we need to stay firm with the decision. Can you imagine a huge ship and the captain keeps changing his mind which way to go? What is going to happen? Chaos, right?

As captain of our ship we make firm decisions and we implement it in a really respectful manner – no yelling, screaming or getting cross with everyone.

Some family members may not like that decision and they are likely to have feelings about it. That's OK – people (including children) have feelings. So, we listen to our children, be there with them. If they are having big feelings because it wasn't the way they wanted it to be, we just stay with them and listen and respect that they need time for those feelings to pass.

Finally, the last part of the verse – **Certainly Allah loves those who put their trust in Him**.

What does it look like to put your trust in Allah?

- Understanding and accepting that everything is by the Qadr (decree) of Allah.

- When parenting is chaotic understand that it is part of the tests from Allah and we don't have to panic or lose it.

- That our children will make mistakes, because we all make mistakes – that's how Allah created us to be.

- And that we can calmly steer our ship through those troubled waters knowing that Allah is there for us and that Allah is going to guide us.

- Always making Dua (supplication) to Allah to guide us in the right directions with our children.

What not putting your trust in Allah feels or looks like:

- Panicking.

- When you look at your child and you see a gloomy future. For example, you see your child hitting another child and you become convinced that your child is turning into a violent person.

- Having panicky, scary, fearful thoughts about what's to come.

That is not putting our trust in Allah because there is absolutely nothing to say from one day to the next that if our child behaves this way today, that means that they are going to be this kind of person and that we need to panic.

The peaceful parenting approach is to see what is happening in this moment and what needs to be done in this moment to get them back on track. It is as simple as that.

Think of our children as little people that we're calling to Islam and give them the same manners we would give a stranger if we're talking to them about Islam – show them the beauty and the passion that we have for it just as we would somebody who we are doing Dawah (calling to Islam) with.

Reflection Points:

1. What behaviours do your children do that really drive you crazy?

2. When your child does that, what does it remind you of? What happened to you as a child when you behaved that way?

3. I am gifting you access to my special program, Parenting For Paradise. You can access it here: www.parentingforparadise.com

To download a complimentary workbook and videos for this chapter go to www.stepupbonus.com

Chapter 6

Am I His Servant?

And we created you in pairs. – Qur'an 78:8

It wasn't right!

I'd been given the task of keeping this team together until we shut down the system and yet everyone wanted to mess with that. I had a different solution, so I marched into my CEO's office, said my piece and walked away pleased that he'd listened and followed my lead.

It was a powerful feeling to be able to walk in to see the person who had the final say in the company, to be listened to and to protect the people who are in my charge. That was my job. It was my job to know what was best for them and to share that leadership role with the CEO, because maybe the CEO didn't always know what was best for my team.

This is exactly the way we should look at marriage.

The verse: **'And women shall have rights similar to the rights against them, according to what is equitable; but men have a degree (of responsibility) over them. And Allah is Exalted in Power, Wise.' – Qur'an 2:228** is often represented as evidence to support that men are superior to women. In fact, in careful reading you can see that is not the case at all. Men are given a degree of responsibility. Just like the CEO had the final say over my team, the husband gets that last decision where agreement isn't reached. With that decision comes the accountability for whether it was, in fact, a just and fair decision based on the right intentions. That means he will be accountable on the Day of Judgement for what he decides.

What this verse really represents is:

- Men and women have similar rights.

- Men have a greater degree of responsibility over the women than that of women over men.

So, his leadership role of protector/guardian does not imply any sort of inequality or dictatorship, also it does not imply any superiority or advantage before the law.

Prophet Muhammad (peace be upon him) said:

The best of you is the best to his family and I am the best among you to my family. – Sahih Ibn Hibban

Islam further emphasises the importance of taking counsel and mutual agreement in family decisions. The Qur'an gives us an example: '**...** **If they (husband and wife) desire to wean the child by mutual consent and (after) consultation, there is no blame on them ...** ' – Qur'an 2:233

We also find in the Qur'an:

They (your wives) are your garment and you are a garment for them. – Qur'an 2:187

This verse of the Qur'an reveals the basic purpose and concept of marriage in Islam. Islam enjoins that a wife and husband should have the most intimate and loving relationship. Each should cover, protect and safeguard the interests of each other. The implications of this verse are:

- Both have an equal status in sharing the responsibilities of marriage.

- A garment is the closest thing to you and therefore the relationship between husband and wife is close and intimate.

- Just as garments protect us from wind, cold and sun, husband and wife are a protection for each other.

- Garments are also a form of beauty and therefore represent the beauty of the relationship a husband and wife share.

So just as I had a leadership role within the IT company I worked for, and the CEO had the top leadership role, wives also have a leadership role within the family.

The Prophet (peace be upon him) was guided directly by Allah, received revelations from Allah, and yet he still listened to his wives, allowed them to show initiative, intelligence and bring solutions to problems. He consulted them and he communicated with them.

We are instructed to be cooperative with our husbands, but that does not mean that we become subservient to them and become their slaves. We are only slaves to Allah. We are still human beings in our own right and we are garments to our husbands as much as they are garments to us. That is the way it should be.

As the mother of my children, I am their leader. Sometimes the father, who's out of the house a lot more than the mother, makes decisions that are not right for his children, because he has not been there in the house and seen everything that is going on. It is our job to step up and explain to him in the most respectful manner that his decision may not work and give him some options and alternatives. Just like I did with my CEO on behalf of my team.

As a respectful leader within the family we do not have these conversations in front of our children, because that is undermining his leadership, just like I would not go to my CEO in front of the team and say something.

We do not undermine the leadership, but we support the leadership with our own leadership. This is what I wish for my sisters as I wish for myself – that you are able to see how much of a leader you are within your own marriage, that you can still be a leader and a cooperative wife, that you can still have your own say without being disrespectful. That comes again from having that inner peace, coming from that neutral, calm space inside and not seeing or judging our husbands for their wrongdoings, but approaching it from a perspective of, 'Maybe he didn't know', giving him the benefit of the doubt and approaching in the most loving and respectful manner. From the perspective of, 'I am his garment and he is mine'.

There is another area that we sometimes get confused when it comes to husbands and the concept of obedience to them, except when what they call for is disobedience to Allah.

The Prophet (peace be upon him) said, 'No obedience in what is sinful. Obedience is only in what is lawful and permissible [agreed upon]'.

So, the question to ask is: 'Are we pleasing our husbands and displeasing Allah?'

Sometimes we lose sight of that, because sometimes we get caught up in the fact that disobeying our husband is displeasing to Allah and we forget to check in whether obeying him may also displease Him.

I will give you an example from my own life.

Back in 1995 there was limited access to Internet, there were no classes that I could attend locally and I didn't have access to books. Any books I did buy were ridiculed by my husband and he prevented me from reading them by saying that I would be led astray by the weak Hadiths that were in them.

The interesting point about that was that by obeying him on that particular matter, I deprived myself of the knowledge and seeking knowledge that Allah requires of each and every one of us, male and female.

I did so because I believed him, only to discover that once I left that marriage and started studying the religion with passion just about every single teacher I came across was using these exact books that he told me not to study. I came to understand that he was keeping me from that knowledge, because that knowledge would empower me and if I became empowered, then I would probably leave.

But that was not the example I was going to give you. The example I was going to give you was how important in Islam it is to be honest.

A companion asked the Prophet (peace be upon him), 'Can a believer be a coward?' He said, 'Yes, he can be coward'. Then it was asked whether a believer could be a miser. He replied, 'Yes, he can be a miser'. It was then asked whether a believer could be a liar. He replied, 'No, a believer cannot be a liar.' – Muwatta Imam Maalik

I found myself lying on behalf of my husband because if I didn't the consequences were horrible. I listened and obeyed and followed his instructions to do things that in my heart and my soul I hated. I was too scared to displease him and in the process I did many things that were displeasing to Allah. May Allah forgive me.

I was so caught up because I was told over and over again that if he went to sleep angry with me then the angels were going to curse me until the morning. If I left the marriage and split up the family, Allah was going to be unhappy with me and punish me. I could not see clearly how wrong it was to give in to his demands on matters so displeasing to Allah. I was so confused.

We are only obedient to our husbands when it comes to continuing to be obedient to Allah. But, if anything that they are requiring of us requires us to be disobedient or displeasing to Allah, then we are not to obey them.

They are human too, and they will make mistakes, as any human will. It is important we fulfil our role as his garment by enjoining the good and forbidding the evil when he has these moments. That is how we show up as a leader in the marriage.

The believers, men and women, are guardians, one of another: they enjoin what is just, and forbid what is evil. – Qur'an 9:71

We have a role to play in marriage that is much more than keeping the house clean and providing nice food and looking after the children. We are an important leader in the family, too.

I love something that was shared with me in my early days as a Muslim. One of the Arab women said to me, 'The husband is the head of the family, but we are the neck. We can turn the head any way we want'. I thought that was rather cute.

Not quite sure it's 100% in line with what we learn in our religion, but it certainly shows us that there is more to being a wife than being submissive to every word of the husband. There is a very sensible middle road that we follow.

May Allah guide us to the straight path.

Reflection Points:

1. Do you respectfully ask for what you need in your marriage or do you stay quiet and grow resentful that you don't have what you need?

2. Are you being his garment, in the true sense?

3. What can you do to make your marriage even better than it is now?

To download a complimentary workbook and videos for this chapter go to www.stepupbonus.com

Chapter 7

Whose Money Is It?

'Money can't buy happiness, but it sure as **** can rent it.'

That was the belief my long-term partner held and what I decided to believe as well. I had worked my way from junior programmer on $23K a year to management on over $100K a year and a company car in less than five years. My hobby was cave diving, as in scuba diving in underwater caves. We bought a house, drove nice cars, travelled to exotic locations to dive in shipwrecks and lived a really affluent lifestyle.

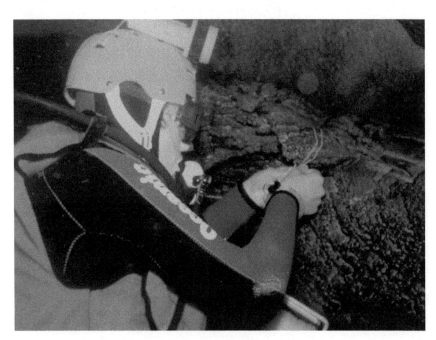

In February 1995, I went on a weekend scuba trip on an old yacht called the Falie. We dived with seals, caught crayfish, drank and enjoyed ourselves. My partner was unable to join this trip because he had to work so I was one of a few women with a group of men. This wasn't anything unusual for me since most of my life I had been in male-dominant environments and I could keep up. I was fit and strong.

Something shifted for me that weekend, though. I didn't behave very well. I was flirtatious and enjoyed the male attention I was getting. I certainly didn't cross any lines of infidelity, but my behaviour left my moral compass feeling really uncomfortable.

This lifestyle wasn't making me happy. In fact, I really felt myself becoming more and more empty. Money was no longer renting happiness for me.

The shift that weekend led me back to some old belief systems around money: that rich people behave badly. When we lived with a rich person and lived a rich lifestyle when I was a child, I was sexually, physically and emotionally abused. When I dated a rich boy in my final year of school he date-raped me. Now I was rich and behaving badly.

I wasn't connecting these dots consciously, this is what I realised was happening in retrospect. At the time, it just looked like I was dissatisfied with my life.

I started exploring other ways to find solace. I went to workshops like 'The Goddess Within'. I carried around gemstones believing that they would shift the energy in my life in positive ways. Anything that would fill the void that had opened up.

In June 1995, I met the Muslim who first introduced me to Islam. I had no idea what Islam was, I had no idea who Muslims were – I was incredibly ignorant. I was curious, though. I watched as he went from a beautiful, somewhat lost soul, to being called back to his religion, start praying, stop drinking, and becoming more calm and purposeful. It intrigued me to watch the change in him. He very gently and kindly kept me at arms-length to fulfil his religious obligations and at the same time shared with me some of the beauty of Islam, including the video by Keith Moore.

Part of his journey of reconnecting with Islam was to also reconnect with his family and he left Australia to return home within a few months of us meeting.

By October 1995, I had embraced Islam as well. From atheism, through new-age spirituality, to Islam in a matter of months.

As you already know, the next stage of my journey was into a marriage that was abusive on all levels, and this included financially.

So, with my new belief that money brought about bad behaviour and my other beliefs about myself that I wasn't deserving or good enough, I was also very vulnerable to being exploited financially.

When my husband declared he couldn't work because of his injury I believed him and happily worked hard to support the family doing contract IT work. I undervalued my worth, was caught up in the false belief that I should be grateful that he married me to keep me strong in Islam and thought that by providing financially for the family I was being worthwhile. I did not have any understanding of the Islamic rulings in regard to financial matters, had no idea about my rights and his obligations. I was creating my own happiness by thinking I was being worthwhile.

I happily paid for everything, including for my two stepsons. I did my best to love them as my own.

We then started a family together and I was trying to work, as well as care for everything. By this time, I came to understand that my husband had a chronic marijuana addiction and that my belongings were gradually being traded for drugs. When those ran out, the pressure was put on me to hand over what I was earning. I had gone from being financially free, living an affluent lifestyle, to being financially abused and living below the poverty line. Despite my quite healthy pay, we had little.

I was tired, working full-time, having children, looking after children, and doing all the cooking, cleaning and driving everyone around while he sat in the shed and smoked our money away.

(This is another lesson in why it is important to understand our religion and to support our new sisters in Islam.)

The purpose of telling this story is to highlight the stories I had around money. At first, money was about renting happiness, then money was evil because it made people behave badly and then earning it gave me self-worth.

Yet the reality is, money has no power at all!

We are the ones that put the power and the pain into money by making up our stories around money.

Money is considered to bring status amongst some.

Money comes across as a right to others.

Money is used to control and manipulate.

Money can be a means to an end.

Whatever it is, each and every one of us has a story around money.

Despite our changing stories around money, things that do not change are the rights that Islam gives women around money. It is really important as women that we understand what those rights are, because quite often money is used to manipulate women within marriage and within work environments. We have already seen in Chapter 2 how women are paid less than men for exactly the same role with exactly the same qualifications.

Islam does not discriminate in a negative way at all when it comes to money, even though some love to twist things and make it look that way.

One such example is around inheritance. Inheritance is a very complex matter and I am not going to, for one second, pretend that I understand the complexities of it, but I do know this:

- When a woman inherits, based on Qur'an 4:11, a female receives half of the inheritance of her male siblings or relatives. However, it should be noted that there are also eleven cases where a woman inherits the same amount as a man, in fourteen cases she inherits more than a man, in five cases she inherits and a man does not, and only in four cases will a woman inherit less than a man. (Sultan, S 1999)

- When she inherits her portion, she spends it in any way she chooses.

- When the male inherits his portion, he must spend it on any family members that are within his care, within his responsibility, including maybe the women that also inherited.

Many like to share the fact that women inherit less than men without adding in the other details and conditions!

We know from our example of Khadejah, the mother of the believers, the first wife of the Prophet (peace be upon him), who was a very powerful businesswoman and quite wealthy, that it is permissible for women to run their own business and for women to have their own wealth.

With such rights also comes responsibilities and there is always a balance in Islam between rights and responsibilities. We have a responsibility as much as the men do to earn any wealth through Halal (lawful) means and to spend it through Halal means. That means that we do not sacrifice our modesty, our practice of our religion or our values in earning an income.

It is reported that the Prophet (peace be upon him) said: **'I stood at the gate of Paradise and saw that the majority of the people who had entered it were poor people, while the rich were kept outside (waiting for their reckoning) … ' – Bukhari and Muslim Hadith**

The phrase 'the rich were kept outside' means that they will be prevented from entering Paradise along with the poor because they will be held accountable for their wealth first. This makes it clear that we will be accountable for our money.

As women, it is important for us firstly to understand some of the most important laws of money/finance in Islam, understand our rights, so others aren't taking advantage of us financially and oppressing us through financial means and to also understand our responsibilities to Allah, to our community and to our family with regards to money. Quite often, as it was in my case, women are manipulated in ways that are unfair and certainly not a part of our religion.

Money is just a vehicle to a destination. Just as we steer the car in the direction we choose, we must also do the same with money. Earn it well and spend it well. Make it a means to earning more reward on the Day of Judgement. That is how you become the leader of money, rather than be controlled by your thinking around it.

Remember, money does not have any control over you. It is only your belief and your thoughts about money that is creating that experience for you.

In fact, look at it this way: If you don't have money, it is good because you have less to be taken account for. If you do have money, it is good because you have something you can spend to earn more reward.

Reminds me of the words of the Prophet (peace be upon him): **'Amazing is the affair of the believer, verily all of his affair is good and this is not for no one except the believer. If something of good/happiness befalls him he is grateful and that is good for him. If something of harm befalls him he is patient and that is good for him.' – Sahih Muslim**

Reflection Points:

1. Do you know about the financial rulings in Islam?

2. What is your story around money?

3. Ponder for a moment about every cent that is coming into your life and every cent that is leaving. If they were to speak, what would they say about their experience with you?

To download a complimentary workbook and videos for this chapter go to www.stepupbonus.com

Chapter 8

When Do I Get A Say?

They did it again!

We had put all this effort into preparing an amazing talk on Muslim women for the open day at the mosque and they expected us to talk about it in the corner, competing with the noise of everyone else presenting their talks at the same time.

It wasn't going to work. It wasn't going to have the impact we had hoped for. Most of all, it was a topic that needed to be spoken about to start debunking the myths out there about Muslim women.

So instead of accepting this, I walked up to a member of the committee and shared my thoughts. Alhamdu Lillah (praise be to Allah), they happily agreed to give us centre-stage to present our talk. We were about to begin using our natural 'teacher' voices when the president of the committee handed us the microphone. They were completely supportive of our suggestion.

All it took was to say something!

How many times have we needed something, wanted something, had an opinion on something and we held back and did not speak up?

During my years in school and university, I was always very involved in committees. I held positions as president, secretary and treasurer. I worked with men and women on different projects. In a very respectful and business-like way we had the voice, opinions and suggestions from both men and women when it came to making decisions. Our projects were very successful.

In the years of being a Muslim I have seen a very different picture. Men run the show and make the decisions and the women complain about it. Not in all cases – there are some good examples out there, but they are the exception, not the norm.

From both perspectives this is not right.

I have not found evidence that suggests women are not allowed to be a part of committees or the decision-making process when it comes to community projects. On the contrary, we have already seen how the Prophet (peace be upon him) consulted women in matters of great importance.

There is clear evidence that talking behind people's backs in a negative fashion is not just bad form, it is strictly forbidden.

If we are to work well as an Ummah (community) then we need to start working together.

This section is not going to be about picking apart men. I truly believe for the most part they just do not realise how their decisions do not work for us because we are not speaking up in a powerful way to tell them. Quite often we expect them to be mind readers and know what it is that we are thinking.

There is also an attitude of 'Why bother, it won't make any difference any-way', and of course, if we don't bother, it definitely won't! I live by the rule, 'If you don't ask, it is a "no" already'.

So, what is going on that is stopping us from taking the lead to change the way things are done in our community?

We are very quick to complain when there are things that are wrong for us and very quick to complain when there are not activities for us. Unless we are stepping up as a community of women and sharing that responsibility of making it a better place for us, how are we ever going to have the things that we are looking for?

We need to be a voice in our community. We need to be the examples we have seen in the time of the Prophet (peace be upon him) who had active roles in the community.

I challenge every Muslim sister who reads this to think about what Allah has blessed you with. What skills, talents, education and experiences do you have that contribute to the community?

Our children need us to step up and make this world a better place for them too. Our children need to have Islamic appropriate activities that they can participate in. We need to have that community time together doing things that are very beneficial, educational and constructive.

Not just eating, socialising and leaving.

I challenge you to step up and step into the community as part of the solution. If we all stepped up imagine what a different world we might have! Remember: many hands make light work. If we did this together it might not be as hard as you think!

This means going beyond establishing a 'women's committee' at the mosque that simply deals with 'women's issues'. Women must be included in the decision-making process in matters that relate to the Ummah in general because it directly affects half of the Muslim community and, many times, all of it. For example, if your mosque or centre is expanding or renovating, few brothers will understand the need for including a baby changing station in a bathroom. A sister is more likely to bring this up.

At the time of the Prophet (peace be upon him), women freely discussed issues that concerned them with him and, later, with other community leaders. They did this inside and outside the mosque. Whatever method they chose, be it public or private, they let their voices be heard.

I go back to the question: What is stopping Muslim women from doing this?

The purpose of this book is to help Muslim women step up as leaders, so I am going to focus on us, not everyone else who may be making it difficult.

The reality is that much of the time we hold ourselves back.

We hold ourselves back because we lack confidence.

We hold ourselves back out of fear.

We hold ourselves back because we don't believe we can make a difference.

We hold ourselves back because we are really creative storytellers and we have created a beautiful story in our head on all the reasons why we can't do it!

Sadly, in doing so, we are missing out on so much.

Every single one of us has been blessed with strengths, skills and abilities that could be earning us great reward on the Day of Judgement.

Access to those rewards is only one thought away!

Reflection Points:

1. Get a piece of paper and pen. Write down everything you are good at, trained in, experienced at.

2. What can you do with these gifts that will benefit the Ummah (community)?

3. When are you going to start?

To download a complimentary workbook and videos for this chapter go to www.stepupbonus.com

Chapter 9

But How?

'You have an inbuilt guidance system, it's called wisdom ... '
— Jamie Smart

I just wanted to get it right.

I knew this was vitally important. I knew inside exactly what it was that I wanted to share, but I could not find the words.

I had been teaching peaceful parenting for a while and now my journey had gone in another direction. I was blessed with understanding the Inside Out Paradigm, the psychological paradigm that brings about fearless confidence, resilience and inner peace.

The things that had changed for me were just beyond words, which is probably why I was struggling to find the right words to teach it to my group.

It was the end of:

'I'm not good enough.'

'I'm not important.'

'I don't matter.'

And all the other limited thoughts that had held me back my entire life.

One of the most exciting changes was being able to say no. If you have never had a problem with saying no it will be hard to understand my excitement at being able to casually say, 'That doesn't work for me, no'. I had been a people pleaser and struggled so hard to make sure everyone was happy. When I realised that it isn't possible to make people happy, I was completely relieved of the need to please people. I was free to choose to please Allah and Allah alone. Alhamdu Lillah (praise be to Allah).

But how was I going to get this concept across to my students?

I picked up the book *The Enlightened Gardener* by Sydney Banks. Sydney being the founder of this understanding, I hoped I would find the answers in his book. Perhaps if I wrote down each part of his explanation I would find the right words.

Every time I was in the car I was listening to lectures by Keith Blevins, my teacher and mentor of the Inside Out Paradigm.

Then I had some questions, so I booked in for a session with Keith to get clarity on what Sydney was talking about in his book.

I was immersing myself in the hope that I would find the words to start teaching this understanding of our psychology.

As I was reading and listening I was gaining more clarity and insight into myself and the paradigm. My attention had been directed away from my own problems and I was focused on how to teach the paradigm. It allowed enough pause between my thoughts for new insight.

I taught my first class.

I totally overwhelmed them with everything in one session. It wasn't well thought out – it was a crazy off-load of everything I had learnt.

After it was over, I felt really tired.

For two days I felt like I was in a fog and all I wanted to do was sleep. It was a strange tiredness. When it lifted it was as if someone had taken off a blindfold from across my eyes and I could see things so much more clearly.

For weeks I was struggling to articulate what had happened. The best way I can describe it is that the mask that I had worn for 46 years, the mask of confidence, the mask of strength, of being superwoman, the amazing person that everybody admired, that mask fell away and what came forward was a fearless confidence to be myself.

It was so refreshing.

I didn't have to sit there and rehearse how I was going to say no. If something didn't work for me, I just said, 'That doesn't work for me'.

I didn't have to think hard about what the other person was going to feel if I stood up for myself and needed something.

I didn't wait for the right moment anymore, because I realised there never is one.

This transformation happened nearly two years ago.

It might seem really strange that, without doing anything to 'fix' all the old thinking I had going on in my mind, it fell away, just … like … that!

That is exactly how insight works!

Here is some of what my students say (in case you thought it was too unreal to be true):

'The understanding of the Inside Out Paradigm has allowed me to live life feeling connected to Allah spiritually and emotionally, which manifests as inner peace, hope and fearless confidence.' – Rayesa Gheewala, USA

'I don't get so caught up in all my thinking anymore. Life is peacefully going by even though to the outside world it looks like I am in crisis.' – *Sajida Sacranie, Ireland*

'The *Inside Out Paradigm* for me is like returning to the Fitrah (natural state), and getting in tune with the innate wellbeing, just as Allah created us. There's no going back.' – *Umm Rayyan, UAE*

'I feel like understanding the Inside Out Paradigm has given me roots and wings: it grounds me in reality with serenity, and helps me see truth and possibilities with more clarity.' – *Maryline David, Ireland*

'I learnt how I function psychologically and that brought for me peace and clarity. I feel emotionally stronger when facing hardship and a lot more patient.' – *Romy Ramos, Australia*

Some of the implications of understanding this paradigm are:

- Feeling confident

- Being resilient throughout whatever is going on around you

- The ability to be patient and compassionate with others

- Having a good relationship despite the other person not changing

- Inner calm despite the turbulence of life

- Deeper connection with Allah

- Non-judgemental thinking around others

- Clarity in life's purpose.

The key reason that these results happen without effort or consciously 'working on' our problems is because they are our natural state of being.

Just look at the persistence, resilience, confidence, patience and inno-cence of a young baby. To learn to walk they have to fall, over and over and over again. Undaunted by the bumps and bruises, they keep going until they master putting one foot in front of the other without falling.

The Prophet (peace be upon him) said, 'Each child is born in a state of "Fitrah", then his parents make him a Jew, Christian or a Zoroastrian ... ' – Bukhari and Muslim

Our natural state (Fitrah) is clarity. Clarity is the pure state of Islam.

So when the stuck thinking falls away, clarity is already there. It is as if you have been wearing glasses that have been distorting the way you see the world and you take them off to see what is really there.

Understanding the implications of the Inside Out Paradigm comes through insight. It isn't something I can just teach you; your understanding will come through your own insight. Like a special lesson made just for you.

What is an insight?

Sight is our ability to see outwardly. We have eyes that take in the infor-mation of what is around us and then build a picture for us to understand our environment and what we see.

Insight comes from within. It is a moment of clarity that comes from within, a blessing from Allah to a greater understanding. It is the gift of heightened consciousness of ourselves, others and all of Allah's creation. As we are blessed with more insight, we are less inclined towards think-ing in the old ways that left us paralysed in fear, insecurities and a sense of lacking.

Insight is where we see something that goes beyond our limited intel-lectual understanding. It comes from Allah. We know this is possible be-cause in this verse we learn how Adam came to understand the creation of Allah:

84

And He taught Adam all the names (of everything) … – Qur'an 2:31

Allah has infinite knowledge and power over everything. He is beyond our imagination – the knowledge, power and wisdom that is possible for us when we open our heart to Allah. When we can see the limitlessness of Allah and what is possible, it becomes natural to put your trust in Allah, accept the Qadr of Allah and rely on Allah rather than His creation.

This insight that we experience is a blessing directly from Allah to understanding our self, others and His creation from a new level of awareness. It is through this awareness that we can see clearly that whatever happens we are OK.

Whatever has happened before has gone.

Whatever is to come is unknown.

We only have this moment right now, and living fully and consciously for the sake of Allah means being present in this moment.

And now the mind becomes quiet.

It is at this point the Nafs (ego) drops away and we can step forward as our best self.

- Confident

- Resilient

- Aware

- Compassionate

- Humble

This is when we can step up and be the best leader in our lives.

The first attribute to being an awesome leader in your life and a leader of the other people in your life is to have clarity about what is really you and what is really them.

What is really going on inside you and how is that affecting your reality of the situation?

What is actually going on for them and how is that affecting their reality of the situation?

When you have clarity, it becomes very clear what it is you are meant to be doing or, as the case may be, not doing.

There is no more urgency to fix things, because sometimes the solution is in allowing it time.

There is no longer a feeling of insecurity and the need to control things.

You can accept that some things are just the way they are and it may not be exactly how you like it or want it, but, Alhamdu Lillah (praise be to Allah), it is exactly how Allah willed it to be and there must be some wisdom behind it.

In our religion, we are told to be patient with the first strike of calamity.

We are told to accept the Qadr of Allah patiently.

We are told, 'Don't get angry'.

We are told to do good, despite others doing evil to us.

We are told to forgive.

We are told to repent.

In the next chapters, we are going to learn how understanding our psychology, understanding the way Allah created us psychologically, is the answer to all of this.

After all of that spiel I am now going to tell you what is at the root of the Inside Out Paradigm.

It is quite simple and has massive implications.

Here it is summed up in one simple sentence …

We are living in the feelings of our thinking in the moment.

Put the book down. Walk away and think about those words.

We are living in the feelings of our thinking in the moment.

Once you are done, come back and we are going to explore the implication to this.

Insha Allah (Allah willing).

> **'When you start to see the power of thought and its relationship to your way of observing life, you will better understand yourself and the world in which you live'. – Sydney Banks**

Reflection Points:

1. Have you ever had an a-ha moment? Can you think of what it was and how that changed the way you looked at that particular situation after that?

2. When you read the words 'We are living in the feelings of our thinking in the moment' did you find those words comforting or confronting?

3. Are there any people, situations or circumstances you find yourself in that you believe need to change in order for you to feel better about the way things are?

To download a complimentary workbook and videos for this chapter go to www.stepupbonus.com

Chapter 10

Leadership or Control?

'If he would just go to school on time everyday then I will be OK!'

That was the story in my head.

Every day was the same battle: getting my son to school.

I was on his case constantly, nagging him, trying to be nice one minute and getting agitated the next.

Nothing was working.

I was fearful of the repercussions if he didn't go to school.

The terse letters from the principal.

The disappointed comments from family members.

I felt a lot of pressure to get him out the door, every ... single ... day.

It was exhausting!

I felt the need to control this situation in order for me to be OK.

Needing to control comes from insecure thoughts and feelings.

Understanding this changed my understanding of myself and made me realise that every time I felt like life was out of control it meant that I had some insecure thinking around something.

It gave me the opportunity to explore what that was, overcome the insecurity and be present in the moment. That made it possible to then step up as a leader in that situation rather than as a 'control freak'.

Often what is happening is we are recalling situations from the past, believing that the current situation is just like that time, projecting forward based on this information and then panicking about what is going to happen.

The reality of this entire scenario is that it is all 'thought in the moment'. We made it up. It isn't real. The panicked, out-of-control feelings are coming from our own thought in the moment and have nothing to do with the situation at all!

Let's go back to the situation with my son.

I know from my knowledge of parenting that the best way to motivate him is to connect with him. I can only do that when I have inner peace and speak with a neutral tone of voice.

The minute I have an undercurrent of feelings going on inside of me, no matter how hard I try to fake it, it comes out in my tone of voice.

When my mind started to imagine the phone calls, letters and text messages I had previously received from the school, the facial expressions of disapproving others in my life and anything else that had happened previously around my son not getting up for school, my frustrated feelings started to rise as I imagined this day turning out the same way.

It was all made up in my head. It wasn't my son who was making me frustrated; it was my frustrated thinking. I know this because there have been just as many days when we have had the same scenario and I have been totally fine.

The interesting side note to this story is that the times that I didn't have frustrated thinking around my son getting up, I woke him in a jovial manner, reminded him kindly and was often surprised to find him ready to go out the door on time.

The key to being a leader is seeing that your feelings are coming from thought in the moment. That our feelings of 'not being OK' are coming from thought. When we cannot see that we are OK then we want to control. When we try to control, we are no longer leading, and we are making matters worse rather than better.

The reality is we are OK. We know that because Allah has told us in the Qur'an:

Allah does not burden a soul beyond that it can bear ... – Qur'an 2:286

If we are not burdened with more than we can bear then it means we are OK.

Sometimes we can't see it or forget.

This helps us understand our need to control, and it also helps us understand the people trying to control us. They are trying to control us because they are unable to see that they are OK.

The implication of this is that we can approach controlling people from a new empowered perspective. We do not need to fear their need to control and instead see where it is they cannot see that they are already OK.

Leadership is not about control because control comes from an unhealthy place inside. It comes from our deep insecurities. It may have come from experiences in the past, confusion, doubts or worries about the future.

Insecurities come from not living in this present moment and being totally present right now.

True leadership, whether it is with our own selves or the people around us, comes from being OK right here, right now in this very moment.

It is not about having to fix anything.

It is not about having to do anything.

It is purely about seeing that you are OK.

And when you are OK, it does not matter whether anything outside of you changes or not; your inner world is safe.

Realising you are OK no matter what is happening around you has the beautiful effect of resilience, patience, confidence and inner peace.

There is nothing to do to be OK because you are OK.

As Muslims, we are truly blessed with the hopeful message of Islam. Allah tells us we are OK in so many different ways. When our heart is open to hearing this message, our faith grows strong and our ability to be the Muslim that Allah asks of us becomes natural.

Nothing happens except by the will of Allah.

Say: 'Nothing shall ever happen to us except what Allah has ordained for us. He is our Protector.' And in Allah let the believers put their trust. – Qur'an 9:51

Allah has our back! He is telling us to trust in that.

My favourite Hadith:

The Messenger of Allah (peace be upon him) said, 'Surely, Allah, The Exalted, said, "Whoever shows enmity to an ally of Mine, I have waged war upon him. My servant does not draw near to Me with anything more beloved to Me than what I have obligated upon him. My servant continues to draw near to Me with the voluntary acts until I love him. Once I love him, I am his hearing with which he hears, his sight with which he sees, his hand with which he grasps, and his foot with which he walks. Were he to ask of Me, I would surely grant it to him. If he were to seek refuge with Me, I would surely protect him."' – Bukhari Hadith

Not only is Allah telling us here that He has our back, He is also telling us exactly how we can earn that protection from Him. He gives us the simple guide to being under His protection constantly.

I found such solace in those words when I was in a battle in the family court system. I knew that all I had to do was keep my faith, supplicate to Allah and keep performing my obligatory acts of worship and as much of additional worship as I could. After that I left it with Allah.

After six years of battles through the court system, the case was closed with a monumental win for my children and me.

Everything eventually falls into place. It has happened for me over and over and over again.

Alhamdu Lillah (praise be to Allah).

The misconception we are faced with today is the belief that we have to do something to be OK. This implies that there is a problem that needs to be fixed. The moment you start telling people, 'You have to do this and then you will be OK', they believe that they are not OK already and that they have a problem that needs to be fixed.

The power of belief is incredible.

They say, 'Seeing is believing'. We 'see' that we are living in our feelings of our thinking in the moment through insight.

Insight is a blessing from Allah. Allah blessed us with the Power of Thought and gave us the ability to be free thinking souls. We use the Power of Thought however we choose and through this we create our own reality of what we are experiencing in the moment.

In short: you are OK, but sometimes you don't think you are.

This is important in terms of leadership because when we can see that we are OK we make good decisions about our own life and the lives of those around us. Our ego does not get in the way and we are able to make our intentions purely for the sake of Allah.

We are able to see clearly what is pleasing and displeasing to Allah.

We are able to be patient that sometimes the solutions will take time.

We are able to be resilient when we are hit with challenges that we did not expect.

We are in a stable place psychologically.

I have already stated that the power of belief is incredible.

Alhamdu Lillah (praise be to Allah). We believe in Allah even though we cannot see Him. We see the signs of His creation and we know that He exists.

We cannot physically 'see' the Inside Out Paradigm either, but we can see the signs that it is the way Allah created us psychologically if we look.

Here is an example:

A lion comes racing towards me looking hungry.

The assumption is that I will feel fear. The other assumption might be that if the lion was not there I would not be feeling fear; therefore this contradicts what I have been saying that feelings come from thought in the moment. It appears that the fear is coming from the lion running towards me.

In this explanation, there have been many assumptions. As humans, we do this a lot. We assume details about a situation and how the people in it must feel and base our reactions and judgements on our own assumptions.

First of all, a lion running towards a person is not necessarily going to bring about a reaction of fear. If that lion happens to be the lion of a lion tamer, then the lion tamer may well look at that lion with delight that that lion is coming towards him, because they have a relationship.

The fact that the lion looks hungry is a matter of interpretation depending on the person. To the lion tamer, it could be feeding time and he has the lion's food ready for him.

For somebody who is not used to lions, their thinking may be that the lion wants to eat them and that they are about to die.

That fearful thinking creates the feelings of fear.

A young child, who may not have any experience of a lion, may look at it as a furry animal that looks huggable and not react fearfully as the lion approaches.

Each person's experience of the lion is coming from their thought in that moment.

Even if it is too quick for us to be consciously aware, it is thought in the moment.

We are only conscious of a small portion of what we think about. We have thousands of thoughts in a day. How many of them do you recollect?

Whatever happens to us, whatever we are feeling in any given moment, is coming from that thought in the moment and nowhere else – no person, no object, no situation, no circumstances are creating our experiences. They are being created by thought in the moment.

When you can truly see that, you are OK.

You are already OK and I am going to keep telling you that, but you are truly able to see that you are OK and live in this present moment when you can see that you are living in the feelings of your thinking in the moment.

When you see that you are OK, you can step into being your best self.

The implication of this is that the situations we find ourselves in do not have the power to dictate how we feel. If we cannot see that in the moment then we lose our sense of psychological safety.

When we can see that, we find ourselves freed from our circumstances or even our memories of the past. We are not suggesting that these circumstances do not happen – we are saying that the circumstances do not have the power to dictate how we feel. None of us actually know how we will feel in any situation until it happens.

This means we feel secure psychologically whatever the situation we find ourselves in and so there is no need for us to control anything. We can be our best self and a good leader for ourselves and others.

Reflection Points:

1. Try not to think too hard about what you have just read. The best way to 'see' it is to let it just sit quietly there and settle. Just like after the storm, the muddy water becomes clear as the mud settles.

2. Do you feel like you need to be in control?

3. As you go about your day, notice how you are feeling and reflect on what you are thinking about. Notice the connection.

To download a complimentary workbook and videos for this chapter go to www.stepupbonus.com

Chapter 11

Who Is The Judge Anyway?

I was standing at the front of the masjid, just in front of the pulpit. There were quite a few visitors for open day at the mosque, sitting on chairs and on the floor, listening intently as my friend and I presented the concept of women in Islam.

I was being my true, authentic, Aussie self. I was sharing my stories in my animated way, arms gesturing here and there, smiling, laughing and joking in the way that I typically do. I felt it was really important to connect with the audience. Break down the barriers between Muslims and non-Muslims. It was an opportunity for them to see that I was just a typical Aussie with a scarf on.

I wasn't intentionally trying to behave in a particular way; I was just being me. The significance of this story is that there were several of the Imams from the community there, the Islamic society committee and members of the faculty of Islamic sciences from the university, including the professor.

Normally I would have been too shy, too nervous, worrying about their judgement. Expecting criticism for being a typical Aussie in front of the audience. But I didn't care anymore. I am who I am and Allah created me like this. I am not trying to be anything that is displeasing to Him by showing my true character and standing in front of people, engaging them in the true message of Allah in my own genuine way.

Do you know what happened?

After being a Muslim for 22 years, I finally stepped up and was my authentic self in front of the community for the first time.

When we had finished, I had several of the leaders of the community come to me and thank me. It was such a learning experience. All these years I had been hiding away for nothing. Hiding away because of fear of being judged.

We spend so much time worrying about what other people think that we forget to worry about what Allah thinks. We get so caught up in how we are perceived by Allah's creation and we forget that Allah created us in this way, that we are His creation. So, why are we pretending and hiding and shrinking away instead of stepping up and being our true, authentic, beautiful selves?

My ability to stand there comfortably without thinking about it came from the realisation that feelings come from thought in the moment. It came from the great insight that I shared with you earlier. I didn't actually plan it like that, it just happened. It was only afterwards that I reflected back and I realised it was so different, that I never would have done that before.

I realised that another layer of what had been holding me back all these years had fallen away, all by itself, without me even working on it. It was gone. And that is exactly how it is and how it works.

I had been hiding all these years and it stemmed from my early days of being a Muslim.

Something that is often done innocently when someone embraces Islam is that they are moulded to be a particular type of Muslim by the Muslims around them. We are given a different name so that we don't have our original name. We are encouraged to behave in a different way so that we are like the Muslims around us. There is an expectation that we reject who we were before. We develop a split personality and confusion around who we are.

We cannot be a good leader if we are not our authentic self.

After many, many years of being known in the community as Khadejah, I claimed back the name Kathryn and did so proudly. It is the name my parents gave me and it is a beautiful name and has a beautiful meaning. There was never anything in Islam that told me I had to change it. By claiming back the name Kathryn, I also claimed myself back and I love being me.

Just as each and every one of us should love being ourselves.

You are perfect and beautiful just the way you are because you are exactly as Allah created you to be.

One of the key implications of the Inside Out Paradigm is that we all have our own separate realities. We are all creating our own experience of what is happening around us. When we understand this concept there are many amazing outcomes. One is that we stop worrying about others' judgement of us.

The implications that we all have separate realities are:

- We are not caught up with the fact that other people don't think the same as us and so we are able to respect and embrace diversity rather than be annoyed and afraid of it.

- We realise that we do not think the same as anyone else and no one else thinks the same as we do. Even if we think it would be better if they thought like us we can let it go because we know it is not possible.

- We are better able to listen and communicate.

The end result is that judgement of others falls away. How can we judge someone when we do not know what is going on in their thoughts?

It really brings us to the point where we know that only Allah can judge a person because only Allah knows what is in their heart, right?

Feelings come from thought in the moment means that each and every one of us are interpreting and experiencing the world in our own separate reality.

This means that no matter how hard you try, you cannot make anyone feel, believe or do anything.

You can certainly try to influence, but their choice to follow has to come from them. The stories of the Prophets (peace be upon them all) are a clear example. They could not inspire everyone to follow them. Allah tells us in the Qur'an:

And say: 'The truth is from your Lord'. Then whosoever wills, let him believe; and whosoever wills, let him disbelieve. – Qur'an 18:29

Guidance to the truth is in the hand of Allah alone and no human being has any share in that, as Allah said to His Messenger (peace be upon him):

Verily, you (O Muhammad) guide not whom you like, but Allah guides whom He wills. And He knows best those who are the guided. – Qur'an 28:56

Understanding that our individual thinking is giving us individual realities means that whenever someone is being highly critical or judgemental of you, they are doing so from their own perceptions and views of you. It is their own reality of you based on their thoughts. It may or may not be anything like your own reality of yourself. This frees you from having to accept their reality as your truth about yourself. You are free to be yourself despite their views of you.

A great way of understanding this came from my teacher when he asked our group, 'Would you believe someone if they said you were purple?'. Unless I had just come out of freezing water and was a shade of purple, of course I would not believe them. So why do we believe people's judgements of us that come from their own perceptions?

It is important to reflect on whether they have a point, but we can do this without getting emotional and therefore with more clarity.

It was a conversation I had with someone who was very close to me that gave me great insight into this implication of separate realities. She was telling me that I think this and I believe that and describing things that showed me a picture, a snippet, of what her perception of me was. Everything she was saying was so bizarre to me because it was so far from my own reality of myself.

This insight helped me realise that if we are walking around constantly trying to please everyone and be pleasing to everyone we are going to go insane because we actually do not know what they are thinking.

It helps us to live by this Hadith of the Prophet (peace be upon him):

Whoever seeks Allah's Pleasure at the expense of people's displeasure, will win Allah's Pleasure and Allah will cause people to be pleased with him. And whoever seeks to please people at the expense of Allah's Displeasure, will win the Displeasure of Allah and Allah will cause people to be displeased with him. – Sahih Ibn Hibban

It is the most freeing realisation that we do not have to conform to everyone's perceptions because the reality is we have no clue what their perceptions are unless they tell us and if they tell us, all we will get is a small picture of what is in their mind in that moment.

It frees us to see our relationships from a very different perspective. Our lives are about pleasing Allah and if others are not pleased with us when we are doing everything according to Allah's laws and within His limits, their feelings are beyond our control. We have no control over whether they will be pleased with us or not. It frees us from being responsible for other people's feelings.

And just as we are freed from the responsibility of their feelings, they too are freed from the responsibility of taking care of our feelings. The only one who is responsible for the way you feel is you!

After years and years and years of being so caught up in this web of pleasing people, of trying to make everyone happy, it all fell away with this insight. It gave me the ability to be able to calmly say in any situation, 'I'm sorry, but that doesn't work for me'. I can say no in a very respectful and caring way.

This is a very key attribute to being good leader for yourself and those around you. If we are saying yes when we mean no, we end up resentful because we are overwhelmed and we place the blame on the other person being unreasonable for asking us. Now that we understand separate realities we can see that this is unfair and unjust.

If you are unable to say no, if you are unable to assess what is good for you, then how can you be a good assessor of what is good for everyone? If we are coming from a perspective of trying to please everyone, we are not actually looking at the situation with clarity about what is actually best in this situation overall. How can we be if our mind is caught up in all these emotions that are around pleasing others and often not pleasing ourselves?

This does not mean we become selfish and we suddenly want to please ourselves. We are able to be in a neutral state where we can look at where things are at now and work out in this moment what is the best step forward.

Sometimes that is to do nothing, sometimes it is to do something, but it comes from a neutral state and so therefore it can be truly for the sake of Allah.

One of the things we do not realise is that many a time we thought we were doing things for the sake of Allah when we were really doing it to make ourselves feel better, or because we wanted to please someone, so therefore our intentions have lost their purity.

Messenger of Allah (peace be upon him) said: 'Allah, may He be blessed and exalted, says: "I am so self-sufficient that I am in no need of having an associate. Thus he who does an action for someone else's sake as well as Mine will have that action renounced by Me to him whom he associated with Me."' – Sahih Muslim

Potentially we could arrive on the Day of Judgement and discover that the scale of good deeds is a lot smaller than we imagined. And just to add a little clarity to that point, look at the verse in the Qur'an where Allah says:

Have you seen the one who takes as his god his own desire? Then would you be responsible for him? – Qur'an 25:43

This is an example of that, isn't it? When we make our intention to please ourselves or to please others, our desires become foremost and we are not doing it to please Allah.

Which brings me back to the initial point …

Who is the judge anyway?

The judge is Allah.

Why do we need to worry about the judgement of others? Our job is not to please them, our job is to please Allah and whether they are pleased or not is between them and Allah. We have no control over that. It is all about separate realities and understanding that each and every one of us is riding our own wave in this life where we are all on our own separate journeys together.

It is quite beautiful really when you look at it like that. The water comprises of all these individual molecules. Each water molecule moves in its own separate way to be a part of the whole big picture of the ocean. Coming together to be waves, to be moving, shifting with the tides, yet as one body of water, but still remaining individual molecules and that is how it is for us as humans as well.

When we can see that we are all living our own separate realities, judgement of each other falls away leaving us with the ability to lead from a sincere and powerful space.

Alhamdu Lillah (praise be to Allah).

Before we leave the topic of separate realities, let's explore what it looks like when we cannot see that everyone has their own reality and why this is a problem:

- When others do not think like us we think that something is wrong with us or something is wrong with them

- We feel that we need to get them to see it from our perspective and wind up frustrated and angry with them when they don't

- We see them as being stubborn and inconsiderate.

- We cannot see any other alternative

- We do not feel OK at all and believe that something has to change in order for us to be OK

- We are also unable to see that they also have their own reality that is their truth

It looks like they are wrong and will not admit it.

Can you see from this how unhelpful our thinking can get when we do not understand that our feelings are coming from our thoughts in the moment?

Many relationships and messy situations could well have been avoided if there was one person in the situation who understood. As my coach would say, 'It just takes one sane person in the room for everything to be OK'. By sane person he meant one person seeing it!

STEP UP — EMBRACE THE LEADER WITHIN

Reflection Points:

1. Next time you find yourself in a disagreement with someone, stop talking and listen. Notice their separate reality? Perhaps it might bring the argument to an end!

2. Next time you feel judged by the words of another person, reflect on the fact that it is their separate reality and notice whether that makes a difference as to whether you take what they say on board or not.

3. When you are next making a decision that affects others and get caught up in trying to find the solution that pleases everyone, stop and reflect on the fact that each individual in the equation is living in their own separate reality and that there may not be a solution to please them all. In that moment, see if you can make the decision that will please Allah.

To download a complimentary workbook and videos for this chapter go to www.stepupbonus.com

Chapter 12

Am I Strong Enough?

> *'Clarity isn't an achievement, it's a*
> *pre-existing condition ... ' – Jamie Smart*

I used to think I was strong. It didn't seem to matter what was thrown at me in life, I survived.

The reality is, I was in survival mode. I was not really living. True strength comes from when you pass through the challenges that you are faced with and you are living as well. You are not just in survival mode.

One of the true blessings of having the insight of feelings come from thought in the moment, and understanding the implications of that in your life, is the ability to be quite resilient through whatever it is that life throws at you. In other words, whatever tests Allah blesses you with.

The more we step up in life the more we are tested, because the tests of this life are about seeing whether we are really committed. This knowledge in itself is a comfort.

One of the things that I realised was that the more resilient I became the harder the tests were. When I realised that was happening it made the tests appear easier. I could see them as tests rather than the world falling apart.

See how that is feelings coming from thought in the moment? The fact that I saw it as a test, something that I was going to make sure I passed, gave me a very different experience from the experience of thinking, 'Why is this always happening to me?'.

The complete mindset shift that you get when you understand that you are experiencing every moment based upon your own thought in the moment gives you the ability to experience everything from fresh eyes every time.

Maybe you have been through something 100 times before a particular way. When you open your mind that it is possible to experience the 101st time in a completely different way, guess what happens? You actually live through it in a completely different way.

There is a particular person in my life who was very difficult to be around, especially given my history of being a people pleaser and this person being someone who is very difficult to please. Every time we met, there had to be this whole checklist of all the reasons why I was such a bad person and, given that I was in such a state that I believed everything everybody thought about me, usually the experience of being together was pretty uncomfortable most of the time, because the scene was set right from the first sentence.

I had been totally apprehensive about meeting her after a long time apart. I was running through scenarios in my head, picturing how disastrous it would be based on my experiences from the past. I wasn't sleeping well and was very nervous about how I was going to handle the situation. I had so many other stressful situations going on and it really felt like having to see her again was the last straw.

This was the story I was making up in my head.

Fortunately, we had one of our Inside Out group coaching calls just before the meeting and we discussed the fact that we do not know how we are going to feel in a situation, that this part of the equation is always incomplete and without it all our imagined future scenarios are incomplete. That made so much sense to me and gave me the opportunity to approach our meeting without expectation or prejudgement about how it was going to turn out. I was able to be with her and experience our relationship from a completely different perspective.

We limit ourselves with our imagination about the future. The future does not exist except in our mind. We truly believe the picture that we paint to the point that we even try to convince others to believe it too.

Along with that comes lots of feelings of anxiety, stress and a great need to control what is going to happen so that we will be OK.

I will give you an example.

Let's say you heard about a friend's child who drowned at the beach. It was a sad accident that rocked the community. While you did not see the incident yourself, you are haunted by the image painted in your mind of their son, who you knew, blue and lifeless on the beach.

Every time your child, a very good swimmer who loves the beach, mentions a trip to the beach you become angry with your child and tell them that they are crazy for suggesting it. The emotional response in the moment comes from a picture you can see vividly in your mind of your own child on the beach blue and lifeless. It is a fictitious picture of the future that you have made up in your own imagination.

Your husband tries to convince you to go as a family to the beach because he can see that your child is really keen. You invest a lot of passionate energy into convincing him of how bad that idea is, sharing with him your vivid image of your imagined future to convince him against the idea.

In this situation, the child is being hurt by the mother's harsh words and criticism, the mother is stressed and anxious at the mention of going to the beach and is so convinced by her own imagined future that she tries to convince her husband to believe it too.

See how damaging this can be?

Sadly, this happens a lot in relationships and children are very often the victims of adults imagined futures!

On the other hand, when we can see that the future is not real and that we have no idea how we will feel in the future, we have much less to think about because we do not find it necessary to imagine future scenarios.

We are quite satisfied that, whatever is written by Allah to happen, He has equipped us with the ability to cope in the moment because He has told us so when He promised He will not burden us with more than we can bear.

This does not mean we do not think about the future. We think about the future knowing that it will unfold according to Allah's plan and not ours and that we do not know how we will be thinking about it in that moment.

That leaves us unburdened by what is to come.

I found this quote to be quite profound and true:

> *'Becoming "awake" involves seeing our confusion more clearly.'* – *Rumi*

The more I could see how confused my thinking was and how confused my perceptions of things were, the more that fell away, the more clarity that came.

The implication of understanding that feelings come from thought in the moment 100% of the time and they come from nowhere else, gives us the strength, resilience and courage that we need to live our life. Not to just survive in our life, but to live it.

The mind is much quieter so we experience deeper understanding of ourselves and others, the verses of the Qur'an and feel a deeper connection to Allah.

True strength is living through the struggles and the difficulties, trusting in Allah, relying upon Allah and continuing to be your best self despite the situation you are in. You are not hiding in excuses.

Are you strong enough to be the leader that you need to be in your life and in the life of the people around you?

Absolutely, it is there within you. It always was.

Perhaps you cannot see it so clearly now and there are confused thoughts getting in the way. When that clarity comes, when that thinking falls away, you will be able to see the strong leader that you are and that has always been there within you.

You may be wondering right now how can it be possible for one to effortlessly transform into a courageous, fearless, confident, resilient and patient person? Perhaps you have a history of anxiety or stress, depression, sadness, or other emotions that have been getting in the way. It may appear unreal that it is possible without actually doing something, without there being some sort of therapy or something where you have to change your thinking to positive thinking, where you have to do this in order to be better. The reason that it is possible is because it is already within you. Transforming means to change from one form to another. The reality is you are already all those characteristics, and it is only a matter of seeing it. No transformation necessary!

Another way of looking at it is that the Inside Out Paradigm is a subtractive psychology. In other words, instead of adding things to think about and do in order for you to be OK, we are saying you are already OK and all the thinking that has been actively getting in the way of you seeing that falls away. You have less to do and less to think about, so it is subtractive psychology.

On top of that, it is not something we actively do … it falls away on its own through insight. Every time you are blessed with new insight into how it works, how you work, thinking that is no longer any use to you falls away.

I will give you an example of what I mean by that.

Once upon a time they believed the world was flat. It was thought that ships that never returned had fallen off the edge of the world. There were all sorts of rituals for good luck performed on vessels to prevent them falling off the end of the world. A lot of thinking was put into how they might save themselves from this plight.

When it was learnt that the world was actually spherical and it was impossible to fall off the edge of it, all the rituals and thinking that was put into each voyage were now no longer needed. It fell away with the new understanding of how the world works.

The other point to the story is that once you see clearly that something is true, you cannot go back to believing it another way. After seeing satellite pictures of the earth, you are unlikely to ever believe it is flat, are you?

The Inside Out Paradigm is the same. Once you can see that it is impossible for your feelings to come from anywhere other than thought in the moment, then you cannot go back to believing otherwise. You might lose sight of it sometimes—we all do—but overall your understanding of it will not go away.

It is at this point that I sometimes get students questioning this based on our understanding that everything comes from Allah. It is a good question! Everything is from Allah and there is nothing about what I am saying that contradicts that. Allah created us, and created us with the ability to think. He gave us the Power of Thought. He also gave us the ability to use thought in any way we choose, he gave us free thinking. This ability to choose for ourselves is how we will come to account on the Day of Judgement. Did we choose right over wrong? Did we choose obedience to Allah over disobedience? How did we use the Power of Thought in this life?

And say: 'The truth is from your Lord'. Then whosoever wills, let him believe; and whosoever wills, let him disbelieve. – Qur'an 18:29

Constantly in the Qur'an Allah is asking us to stop and reflect. Asking us to see deeper into what He is telling us. Questioning us.

This is a blessed Book which We have revealed to you, [O Muhammad], that they might reflect upon its verses and that those of understanding would be reminded. – Qur'an 38:29

Why is He doing so?

When we slow down our thinking to a reflective state, 'Stop and smell the roses' as they say, we allow the opportunity for insight and for wisdom to come from Allah.

Say: 'O you mankind! Now truth has come to you from your Lord. So whosoever receives guidance, he does so for the good of his own self; and whosoever goes astray, he does so to his own loss; and I am not (set) over you as a Wakeel (disposer of affairs to oblige you for guidance)'. – Qur'an 10:108

Most of the time, we are not seeing it or hearing it because our mind is running a mile a minute. There is so much chatter going on that we cannot hear over it. There is no room for insight, for us to notice that Allah is guiding us. And yet, every day, we ask Allah to guide us to the straight path in our prayer. We ask and we are not listening! Subhan Allah (glory be to Allah).

The way we are feeling and experiencing everything is through thought. It is not possible any other way. When you take away what is not possible, the simplicity of possibility is all encompassing. It opens the door to truly accepting that anything is possible for Allah, so there really is nothing to worry about in this worldly life.

We are OK!

Reflection Points:

1. Next time you are stressing about something that you are about to do or something that is about to happen, stop and notice the picture you are creating around the future.

2. Can you see that there is nothing to say that the future is going to be as you imagine it?

3. Can you see that you are inherently OK?

To download a complimentary workbook and videos for this chapter go to www.stepupbonus.com

Chapter 13

Can You Be Patient With The First Strike Of Calamity?

Patience can be a really confusing topic, especially if you are someone who has a history of being around controlling people or have been in abusive relationships or around very dominant personalities. We often believe that patience is tolerating their controlling, abusive manner.

I was fortunate enough to have a lesson from one of my teachers on good and bad patience and until that moment I had not even realised there was such a thing as bad patience.

There is, because when we are being patient with somebody's behaviour that is transgressing the limits that Allah has set, we are not actually helping them or ourselves.

We have been told to enjoin the good and forbid the evil:

The Prophet (peace be upon him) said: 'Whoever among you sees an evil action, let him change it with his hand [by taking action]; and if he cannot, then with his tongue [by speaking out]; and if he cannot, then with his heart [by feeling that it is wrong] – and that is the weakest of faith'. – Sahih Muslim

If we are being patient with someone who is behaving in a manner that is displeasing to Allah—as in we are quietly accepting it—then our patience is actually condoning that behaviour. We are enabling them. This is not really patience.

Yet we often feel powerless to do something about it. We feel that, somehow, we are not strong enough or we are not able to be a part of positive change.

I want to define patience before we delve into the topic of patience to make sure that we understand what we are talking about. Patience is not standing there and letting people abuse you. Patience is not about allowing somebody to take your rights. Patience is not about reacting in a bad way in return, in reciprocation for another's bad behaviour either.

Patience is being able to stand there firmly and say, 'That's not OK'.

We are not responsible for the outcome; that is between them and Allah. We are only responsible for doing our bit and doing it in the manner that is pleasing to Allah. They may have an emotional reaction to what we do or say. That is OK. As long as we have fulfilled our duty to Allah in a manner pleasing to Him, we are not at fault and nor are we responsible for their feelings. They are!

When somebody is doing something that is displeasing to Allah then our responsibility is to do what we can about that and we do it in a firm, respectful manner, whether it is as a parent correcting a child, whether it is a wife correcting a husband, whether it is a daughter correcting a parent, whether it is an employee correcting a CEO. Whatever the situation, age, gender, nationality and station in life are not barriers.

Culturally that can be really challenging, because there are people who believe that they have the right to not be corrected. To date I have not found any evidence whatsoever in the Qur'an or the Hadith that supports this view.

'The true source of leadership resides in clarity of mind and clarity of understanding, giving you what you need in the moment to deal with the matter at hand.' – Jamie Smart

When we are talking about leadership and patience, what we are talking about is having clarity of mind and clarity of understanding so that in any given moment, whatever comes up, we are able to deal with it, without an exaggerated or emotional reaction. What is primarily on our mind is what would please Allah. Our internal calm is not shattered; we are in charge of the situation from the first instance.

The Prophet (peace be upon him) passed by a woman who was weeping next to a grave. The Prophet said, 'Be mindful of Allah and be patient'. She said, 'Go away from me! You have not been afflicted by a calamity like mine,' and she did not recognise him. Then, she was told that it was the Prophet, so she went to the Prophet's house and she did not find any guards there. She said to him, 'I did not recognise you'. The Prophet said, 'Verily, patience is at the first strike'. – Bukhari and Muslim Hadith

When we hear the stories of the Prophets and Messengers and what they have been through we often think about how patient they were.

Prophet Yusuf's (peace be upon him) brothers threw him in a well and left him. He also spent time imprisoned unjustly.

Prophet Yunus (peace be upon him) was trapped inside a whale.

Prophet Ayub (peace be upon him) lost everything, one thing after another. His house, his children, his wealth, his health and then eventually his own wife and yet he remained patient.

We think, 'I could never do that. They are obviously extraordinary people and it is not possible for us to be able to be like that, at that level where you are patient with the first strike of calamity'.

The truth is we can.

Certainly, they were extraordinary people. Allah has already told us that they are the best of humankind. They are our role models, our examples.

There are so many stories of the companions of the Prophet (peace be upon him) that also show extraordinary patience that help us see that it is possible for us, too.

Remember the power of belief: If you believe you can't, then you won't!

Here is a story that reminds us that we can:

One of the sons of Abu Talha became sick and died and at that time Abu Talha was not home. When his wife saw that her son was dead, she prepared him (washed and shrouded him) and placed him somewhere in the house. When Abu Talha came home, he asked, 'How is the boy?'. She said, 'The child is quiet and I hope he is in peace'. She prepared food for him, and spent a beautiful night with him. In the morning, Abu Talha took a bath and when he intended to go out, she told him that his son had died.

It is said that Abu Talha was upset that she had kept it from him and consulted the Prophet (peace be upon him) about it after the dawn prayer. The Prophet was complimentary of Abu Talha's wife's actions. He understood that she had wanted to make sure her husband was in the best condition to hear the news of their son.

The Prophet (peace be upon him) supplicated for their night together to be blessed, and the story concludes that they had a son who then had nine sons who all memorised the Qur'an.

I chose this example because I want you for a moment to imagine being a mother and your child has just died of an illness while your husband is away. Instead of sinking into misery, she prepared the child's body and then prepared for the return of her husband so she could prepare him to receive the news in the best condition. This is a beautiful example of patience at the first strike of calamity and evidence that each and every one of us is capable of it.

Patience with the first strike of calamity comes from the clarity of mind and the clarity of understanding we have. When we understand our religion properly, we understand that anything that befalls us happens by the Will of Allah. We understand that anything that befalls us was never going to miss us and anything that we missed out on was never going to be written for us.

That is called the acceptance of the Qadr (Decree) of Allah.

When we understand that after difficulty comes ease, we become patient with the difficulty.

When we understand that Allah does not burden us with more than we can bear, we know we can bear it and we find the patience to bear it.

This is why knowledge of Islam is so very important. Then with the clarity that our feelings are coming from thought in the moment, put the two together and we are able to be patient with the first strike of calamity.

'Inner peace is your natural state.' – Mamoon Yusaf

Our natural state is to be at peace. If we are not at peace we are not in our natural state.

What does it mean, 'our natural state'? Why is this a positive thing to understand?

Let's look at an elastic band. An elastic band has its natural state, the natural shape that it is. If we stretch it and stretch it and stretch it and then we let it go, it comes back to its natural state. If inner peace is our natural state, then this is what we come back to when we stop the stretch. The stretch is all that thought that is going on in our mind that is distracting us.

Like in this Hadith:

The example of a believer is that of a fresh tender plant; from whatever direction the wind comes, it bends it, but when the wind quietens down, the plant becomes straight again ... –Sahih Bukhari

We get pushed and pulled by the tests, the tribulations and the challenges that are brought before us, but when they fall away, when the ease comes after the difficulty, we return back to our natural state: peace!

That is the state of the true believer and that is true resilience. While the wind might be pushing us this way and that way and bending us out of shape, we are still that same plant, green and lush. No matter what way the wind pushes us, inside is still the same. It doesn't move, it doesn't change; it remains strong and resilient despite the wind, which is what gives it the ability to come back to its original state once the wind has gone.

To me, that is being patient with the first strike of calamity. It is to not react or overreact the minute something happens. It is not to wail and scream and cry and then a few minutes later think, 'Oh, I'd better be patient now'.

It is actually striving through each challenge.

Does this mean that we don't have feelings?

Of course not!

There is nothing about what I have taught you so far that says we don't have feelings. Of course we have feelings. That is how Allah created us.

The point is we understand where our feelings are coming from and they are coming from thought in the moment.

I will give you another example that really sums this up. It really sums up the notion of patience with the first strike of calamity, but still having feelings and taking it all into context about having both the knowledge and clarity.

My fifth child was named Sarah.

At thirteen weeks, I had some bleeding and I knew that my husband was really keen for this child. Normally when I supplicate to Allah I leave everything open to Allah. I am not sure why in this particular moment my supplication was very specific, but I asked Allah to save her. I asked Allah to save this baby. Normally I would not make such a specific supplication, but I did in this moment, and it was a beautiful life lesson.

At nineteen weeks, we went for the ultrasound and we knew something was wrong when the radiologist wasn't saying anything. We were taken to an interview room and then the doctor and a specialist were brought in. Sarah had spina bifida and she had no kidneys and she was never going to be able to live outside of me. Of course, there was always this little hope inside of me that maybe they were wrong and, because of our religious beliefs, it was my responsibility to keep the pregnancy to term. My life was not in danger, so therefore I had no right in Islam to take her life. And so, from week nineteen to week thirty-four, I lived with this mixed feeling of what this would mean. I became more and more uncomfortable physically and the natural feeling of 'I just want to give birth to be comfortable again' that most women would feel at this stage of pregnancy was really entwined with feelings of sadness knowing that I was going to give birth to her and she would die.

We had to book her in for a caesarean, because, with the spina bifida, she was always paralysed so she was feet down. The swelling of her head from spina bifida meant she was a risk for me to deliver normally since I had previously had a C-section.

The doctor said there was no choice. We had to book her in for a caesarean and it had to be well before the due date, because they couldn't risk my life by allowing me to go into labour.

I found all of this experience very interesting because it came from a position of knowledge. I understood that the Prophet (peace be upon him) had said look to those who have less than you and so I knew someone who had a child that was severely disabled and was in her thirties and the mother had to care for her constantly. She was still in nappies, she still needed to be hand-fed and I knew that if I had a child like this, this was something that I probably would not cope with very well. So, in fact, I was truly blessed by the fact that I was not going to have a child that I would have to care for to that level.

I could already see that positively and be grateful for what Allah had blessed me with.

Secondly, I understood that the children that die before puberty go to Paradise and they get to call for their parents to join them. So I could see the blessing in it and I knew that if she had lived in this life it would have been a very uncomfortable life for her and yet instead she was going to be playing under trees with the Prophet Ibrahim (peace be upon him). This knowledge gave me the strength to see the whole experience from a very positive light.

She was born, the Qur'an was playing, the Adhan was whispered in her ear, she was given a bit of chewed date; all the Sunnah was performed at her birth. She was passed from one sibling to the other, everyone in the family gave her a cuddle, she was put back in my arms and, after one hour and five minutes of life, her soul drifted away.

It was a really interesting moment because her lungs were never properly developed, so you couldn't really tell she was breathing at all, but I could sense when she drifted away. I just felt it.

This was first thing in the morning, because that is when I was booked in. The Imam came up and washed and shrouded her. We managed to get police clearance for her to be taken from the hospital. She had her Janazah (funeral prayer) and was buried that very same day. The nursing staff came to talk to me and said how beautiful they found the whole experience. There wasn't a dry eye in the room when she was born. They felt at rest knowing that this child had been put to rest that very same day. By the time they left their shift, she was buried.

I then began my four days in hospital. Because it was a caesarean I couldn't go straight home. People came from everywhere from within the community. I didn't even know how they all knew what was going on, but they came. The sisters would sit with me, we would cry, they would walk away. They would come; I would sit with them, tell them the story again, we would cry together and walk away. It was peaceful, sad crying – the way we are permitted to grieve the loss of someone close to us.

After day three, I felt like it was time to go home and get back to my life. I truly understand the Islamic grieving process. We are given three days to grieve and then we must return to our regular routines. The Prophet (peace be upon him) shed tears when his baby Ibrahim died in his arms. I wasn't doing anything wrong by having feelings and crying. I was there, very present in the moment. I was crying a very peaceful, healing cry, not a desperate wail. I never felt a depressive, overwhelming feeling about her death; I had total acceptance and inner calm the whole time.

I have never been depressed by what happened. I have always looked at this experience as the most beautiful experience. Yes, I can find a tear when I think about that very moment when she passed away in my arms. Those feelings coming from that thought in that moment, but I have never felt depressed about it. I have always felt very blessed and grateful to have had her.

For me, this is such a beautiful reminder and story of patience with the first strike of calamity and how the understanding of our religion, the clarity of understanding and also the clarity of mind and being present in the moment helps us be patient.

No matter what we are faced with.

Alhamdu Lillah (praise be to Allah).

Reflection Points:

1. What are you taking away from your journey reading this book?

2. Did you find yourself discovering new things about yourself, what were they?

3. What is your next step going to be? Remember you just have to take that first step ... then trust in the rest of the journey.

To download a complimentary workbook and videos for this chapter go to www.stepupbonus.com

Chapter 14

Inferiority or In-FEAR-iority?

> '*Until we face the real cause of fear – our thinking and the unhealthy way we use it – we will have zero control over fear.*'
> *– Joseph Bailey*

There was a crazy time in my business journey where I was having sales call after sales call after sales call and I wasn't making any sales. I had piles of notes of all the people I had spoken to and yet I was lacking clients.

Something was not right, so my coach took me through an exercise of listening to me and role-playing the sales call. He told me that my voice became robotic the minute I started talking about money.

I realised that there was something going on in that moment that had me changing the dynamic of how I was showing up in the call. Until that moment on the call the people I was working with were feeling on the edge of their seat, feeling really connected, because I am really good at helping people feel safe and listened to, but the minute I spoke about money, that was it. There was a disconnect and the disconnect came because underneath there were feelings and fearful thinking going on quite subconsciously, that had changed the tone in my voice and had the person at the other end doubting me.

Since then I have had this huge shift because I certainly would not be in business still if I hadn't. I love the sales calls now. I don't have a problem talking about money now.

I came to realise that underneath the whole money issue for me was a whole bunch of fears. One of the fears I had was would I be good enough to be delivering what I was offering to my clients?

This is a ridiculous fear, because all the feedback I was getting was that I was delivering something they were finding very valuable. So, it was my own message, my own thinking, my own story that was going on that was sabotaging the whole process. I had a bit of an inferiority complex, but it's not inferiority, it's actually fear. It was fear of not being good enough, fear of not being able to deliver, fear of success. I wasn't scared of failure; I was pretty good at failing!

> *'If the only thing people learned was not to be afraid of their experience, that alone would change the world' –*
> *Sydney Banks*

One of the interesting things that we come to realise the more we understand that we are creating our own experience through thought in the moment is that we are also our own worst oppressors.

We believe that people are oppressing us, by situations and by circumstances. There is real oppression out there, but what I want to cover in this chapter is that the biggest oppression we face is the oppression of our own selves.

O My servants! I have forbidden oppression for Myself, and I have made it forbidden amongst you, so do not oppress one another … –Sahih Muslim

We talk about how it is not OK to oppress each other, but I want to really address the oppression of ourselves, because some of what we perceive and see as others oppressing us is actually our own thought in the moment. The reason I can tell you that with such clarity and such confidence is because that has been exactly my experience.

I believed that the reason I had certain struggles was because people were oppressing me or I was in an oppressive situation. The reality was my own thinking was causing my own oppression. I was building my own cage and I was putting myself in that cage, locking the door and throwing away the key. No one else was doing it to me; I was doing it to my own self. We see this happen a lot. When we've had something happen in the past and it was something that was difficult or hurtful or something that we really struggled with at the time, whenever we have to approach a similar situation or we suspect that we might be having to face something like that again, we stick ourselves in our own cage and build a story around what is going to happen.

Let me give you an example so you know what I'm talking about.

One of my favourite examples is in parenting, because I see this a lot in my work as a parenting coach.

As mothers, we often feel like we are being oppressed by the behaviour of our children and we are being oppressed by those around us who are critical of us about our children's behaviour. We might decide we cannot have a life while our children are this age because of their behaviour, that we have to stay home, not attend classes, and usually become lonely, depressed and frustrated.

The reality is that what is going on is our own feeling coming from thought in the moment, but it looks like it is the children's behaviour that is the problem.

Let's go back to the story of my son not going to school. I felt an immense pressure and really believed that all my stress and anxiety, and even the car accident I had one day, was because my son wouldn't get up for school. I was holding myself hostage in constant thinking that I will not be OK until he gets his act together.

The reason this was oppression of my own self was because the ultimate oppression of our selves is committing sin. My feelings were coming from fearful thinking. I was caught up with what everyone would say or do and how I would come out of it without being embarrassed and judged as a bad mother that I couldn't see that my behaviour towards my son was oppressing him.

We don't want to take this lightly. Allah has forbidden oppression on Himself first!

I put all the blame on my son and then I was putting all this pressure on him and that pressure was pushing him away and making it harder for him to get himself back on track. In fact, my behaviour towards him had him feeling like he wanted to leave home because everyone in his life was 'hating on him' (they are his words).

I am not suggesting I used bad language or caused him physical harm. What I was doing was adding to the problem with my tension and stress and putting the blame on him.

Even when I was trying so hard not to use blaming language, the tone of voice and the manner in which I spoke to him made it very loud and clear what I thought.

When I had an opportunity to untangle what was going on in my head with my coach, I was almost in tears at how harsh I had been on him. I had not been patient and supportive at a time when he needed that from me most.

The oppression I was experiencing was not from the school, the oppression I was experiencing was not from the people in my life, and it wasn't from the judgement that I thought was coming from teachers. The oppression was coming from my own thought around that and my own insecurities of how I would deal with it if I did end up getting a letter from the school, if I did end up facing a fine or court for his absences.

I had built a massive picture in my mind of how devastating it was going to be if my son did not just snap out of it, get to school every single day, get his assignments in on time and do exactly what he was told.

It was all coming from inside me.

My son is still struggling with his health, he is still struggling to attend school, and despite that he is working towards completing his school certificate and graduating from school. The more I pulled back from pressuring him the freer he became to find good solutions for himself. By adding to his stress, I was keeping him from being able to think clearly about his future and find a good solution.

When we are oppressing ourselves through our own fears, we are not leading; we are trying to control. When we try to control we cross the limits set by Allah and oppress others.

By stepping out of my own way, I stepped out of my son's way and he was able to take lead in his own life, approach his teachers and find a way to manage his education well.

This is just an example to show how important it is for us to understand that the experience we are having in a situation is our own creation, that we are developing our own perception of what is happening. I am not saying that it is not happening. What I am saying is the way we are experiencing what is happening is our own creation through thought in the moment.

One of the interesting things about the example I just gave you is how much we believe the story of what is going to happen in the future and how we are behaving in a way that is to try and prevent that.

The only one who knows the future is Allah.

No one in the heavens or earth knows the unseen except Allah. – Qur'an 27:65

The unseen includes the future.

Just because something has happened one way before, it does not mean it is going to happen the same way in the future, because every single time we experience something, we can experience it in a completely different way.

Seeing this as true opens the opportunity to experience it differently and also means we do not feel insecure. Whatever the future is, whatever the truth of the matter is, we can handle it!

A fascinating observation about fearing what will happen in the future is that we actually fear how we are going to feel in that moment.

Pause on that for a moment.

We fear how we are going to feel.

Spelt out like this it seems a little insane.

In fact, it is!

We do not know what we will be thinking in any given moment, so we have no clue how we will feel, so fearing something that is not yet real is fearing our own thoughts. They are only thoughts. They have no life of their own; they are neutral, until we put life into them. We are creating them in our own mind via the Power of Thought.

Essentially what we are doing is similar to drawing a picture of a monster on a piece of paper, then looking at it and being scared of the monster we drew ourselves.

Sometimes the fear of our own feelings is from revisiting in our mind traumatic past experiences. We can imagine our self in the situation and feel the feelings as if we are living it all over again. The reality is that we are not experiencing it again. Whatever it was that happened is no longer happening. What we are experiencing is thought in the moment.

When we can't see that it is feelings coming from thought in the moment, we keep reliving it and we keep giving life back to that trauma.

This may seem too simple, especially with the message out there that therapy and all sorts of other healing is needed to 'get over' trauma. The truth is that it is possible to be OK without any of these things when you can see that it is feelings coming from thought in the moment. As soon as we see that, we are taking the power away from that thought and do not have to relive that trauma over again.

You have learnt about some of the experiences I have been through and I can attest to the fact that this is true. I am no longer traumatised by anything that has happened to me. I am safe and secure. I am OK.

Oppression of our own selves, by being in a state of outside in thinking, as we like to call it, happens to us all, even those of us who understand and can see that feelings come from thought in the moment. We all have moments where we can't see it. We're all human and we all make mistakes. We all go off track sometimes.

That is a good thing, because if we did not have these moments we would probably lose our compassion for others. By having moments where we are reminded of what it is like to lose sight of feelings coming from thought in the moment helps humble us and helps us to be compassionate towards those who do wrong against us or wrong against others. Understanding that someone has acted because they could not see that their feelings were coming from thought in the moment helps. We know that they truly believed that they needed to do something in order to feel OK.

Their actions are not innocent and of course there are always consequences for our actions. Psychologically they were innocent, because they did not realise that those actions were not going to solve the problem.

Psychological innocence opens the opportunity for compassion, for forgiveness, for healing. It allows opportunity for the wrongdoer to repent and correct themselves, which is, of course, the ideal scenario.

People are more likely to actually change their ways, to turn to good, if they are given a non-judgemental, compassionate hand, held out to say, 'Here we are, you can do this, we are here for you'.

Look at our example of the Prophet (peace be upon him). He was the perfect example of this. He gave people the chance to repent. An example is this story:

Anas reported that a Jewess came to Allah's Messenger with poisoned mutton and he took of that what had been brought to him. (When the effect of this poison was felt by him) he called for her and asked her about that, whereupon she said: 'I had determined to kill you'. Thereupon he said: 'Allah will never give you the power to do it'. He (the narrator) said that they (the companion's of the Prophet) said: 'Should we not kill her?' Thereupon he said: 'No'. He (Anas) said: 'I felt (the effects of this poison) on the uvula of Allah's Messenger'. – Muslim Hadith

As is obvious from the above Hadith, the woman openly admitted her assassination attempt on him. His own companions readily offered to immediately execute justice upon her in compensation for the crime. Yet the Prophet let her live.

Everyone deserves the opportunity to repent. Allah does not hold this back from us at any time. We have until the last breath, the last gargle from our throat, to repent for what we have done.

When our fears fade away, compassion for our self and others emerge. Self-correction, repentance and stepping into your best self become effortless.

Seeing that our feelings are coming from our thinking in the moment frees us from our oppression of ourselves and others. We are free to live with fearless confidence, resilience and inner peace.

Life becomes hopeful.

Reformation becomes possible.

Repentance is natural.

Contentment, purpose and passion for living are inevitable.

Alhamdu Lillah (praise be to Allah).

Reflection Points:

1. Are you being oppressed? Reflect and see if your circumstances or others are really oppressing you, or if are you oppressing yourself through your own thoughts.

2. Is there anyone in your life who you are being harsh and judgemental to?

3. Having read the book this far, what can you see that is still holding you back from stepping up and embracing the leader within you?

To download a complimentary workbook and videos for this chapter go to www.stepupbonus.com

Chapter 15

Am I Enough?

> *'It's your road and yours alone. Others may walk it with you, but no one can walk it for you.' – Rumi*

Yes!

And that is exactly what this is about. Each and every one of you is a leader. Each and every one of you is perfect and beautiful just the way you are. You may not believe it yet, but I am hoping that through this book you have gradually been able to see the possibilities.

You may not be able to see how you can be strong, patient, resilient, courageous, fearless and confident and that is OK. It is your journey and you are walking your journey at your pace and you will get to where you are going at your own speed.

Success is by putting one foot in front of the other. Eventually, insha Allah (Allah willing), you will get there. I want to remind you that the best thing you can do moving forward from here is to make the intention that you want to be your best self for the sake of Allah. Use the time on your prayer mat when your head is in Sujud (prostration) to ask Allah to help you on that journey. Ask that Allah grant you access to the resources, the people, the time and everything that you need to achieve that. That Allah blesses you with clarity, blesses you with the truth, blesses you with the possibility of living your life rather than just surviving it.

'Don't let the noise of others' opinions drown out your own inner voice. And, most important, have courage to follow your heart and intuition. They somehow already know what you truly want to become. Everything else is secondary.' – Steve Jobs

Every time you find yourself at a barrier, at a hiccup, a road bump on the way, ask Allah. Always put your trust in Allah. Every single time I have not known what to do next, I have just had one simple request of Allah. It does not come with complicated words, it does not come with a particular prescription – it is really simple. I just ask Allah to help me. The reason I make it so simple is that Allah knows best. Allah knows better what is good for me than I do for myself. I don't want to be so specific that I limit the options, because I know that my intelligence, the intellect, the knowledge and the wisdom that Allah has blessed me with is limited. It is just a drop in the ocean compared to what Allah has to offer, so why close my mind and my heart to something greater than me? That is exactly the same approach to take to what I have taught you through this book.

If you try to figure it out intellectually, if you try to nut it all out and put it all together and figure out how this works here and this works there and fill your head with all this thinking, you are not going to be in the quiet space where insight will come to you. You will not be able to see clearly what it is about.

We have access to immense blessings from Allah. All our knowledge, all our wisdom, all our thought – everything about us comes from Allah. If we open our heart and mind to the potential and opportunity of that, we have the opportunity to live our life really pleasing Allah and with a good connection to Allah.

I would like to conclude the book with a beautiful story. I was so blessed in 2013 to be invited to go to Hajj (pilgrimage).

It was the most incredible experience. Being in a sea of Muslims from across the globe, literally millions of people all in one place, praying together in complete harmony, was the most amazing picture of what is possible for the human race. It really was.

As I did the Tawaf (circumambulation of the Kabah), tears pouring down my cheeks, I really felt the connection with Allah. I felt that true repentance for all that I had done wrong. I felt the absolute desire to do more for the sake of Allah. I never wanted to leave. I did not want to leave that feeling. Then on the day of Arafat, supplicating to Allah and knowing how Allah answers our supplications on that day, again, the tears streamed down my cheeks. All I could do was open my heart to Allah and feel the beautiful connection.

Then to spend some relaxing, calm, quiet days in the tranquillity of Medina, the home of our Prophet (peace be upon him); to witness where the Sahaba (companions of the Prophet) were buried and imagine having lived amongst them; visiting Mount Uhud and imagining the battle – I did not want to leave. I did not want to leave because I truly believed at the time that I had to be in those places to experience that feeling.

To experience that closeness to Allah.

To really feel that true repentance.

To really feel the love of Allah.

To really feel that passion about what I am doing moving forward.

A few years later I learnt about the Inside Out Paradigm and started my journey to being the person that I am today.

One night, sometime in the middle of the night, I felt inspired to pray. I was standing in my lounge room on a dirty carpet that had breadcrumbs and all sorts on it. It really needed a good vacuum. Feeling the tears falling down my cheeks and feeling that real connection with Allah, that true repentance and that passion in doing more to please Him, I realised: I didn't need to be on Hajj to have that feeling again. I could have that feeling any time, at any moment, in any place. That feeling, that connection to Allah, comes from our own thought in the moment.

The Prophet (peace be upon him) said, 'Allah the Most High said, "I am as My servant thinks I am. I am with him when he mentions Me. If he mentions Me to himself, I mention him to Myself; and if he mentions Me in an assembly, I mention him in an assembly greater than it. If he draws near to Me a hand's length, I draw near to him an arm's length. And if he comes to Me walking, I go to him at speed."' – Sahih Bukhari

Our experience of Allah comes from our own thought in the moment. Allah blessed us with the Power of Thought, but He also blessed us with free-thinking.

He blessed us with the ability to choose how we use that Power of Thought. Our view of Allah will be as we think it would be. That means it is possible to have that connection and closeness with Allah at any moment, because Allah never went anywhere.

We stopped looking for him. We just stopped thinking about him. We are the ones that lose sight, never once did Allah lose sight of us.

I leave you with this note:

Your life can be as you dream it to be. You are a beautiful leader; the leader is within you. You can lead your life in whichever direction you wish it to go. Does that mean that the outcomes and experiences will be the ones that you want? Not necessarily. The way you experience them will be exactly how you choose to experience them and that makes every single experience that you have on this earth amazing, wonderful, exciting and it makes the future look bright, no matter what is ahead of us.

We are so blessed to be Muslim, as we know in the Hadith

The Prophet (peace be upon him) said:

Strange are the ways of a believer for there is good in every affair of his and this is not the case with anyone else except in the case of a believer for if he has an occasion to feel delight, he thanks Allah, thus there is a good for him in it, and if he gets into trouble and shows resignation (endures into patiently), there is good for him in it. – Sahih Muslim

I sincerely hope you continue this journey, learning more about how you can really see that feelings come from thought in the moment, that you continue your journey to inner calm, fearless confidence and total resilience, to be able to step up and be the leader and embrace the leader that is within you.

It has been my utmost pleasure and honour to be able to share with you what has totally changed my life and I pray to Allah with all my heart that you will understand that feelings come from thought in the moment and that transforms your life to be one filled with happiness, despite everything and anything you go through.

Reflection Points:

1. What are you taking away from this book?

2. Is there an area of your life you are not happy with? What is it?

3. What are you going to do about it?

To download a complimentary workbook and videos for this chapter go to www.stepupbonus.com

References

Al-Shifa bint Abdullah **n.d. Foundation for Science, Technology and Civilisation,** http://www.muslimheritage.com/scholars/al-shifa-bint-abdullah

Arwa al-Sulayhi 2017, Wikipedia, https://en.wikipedia.org/wiki/Arwa_al-Sulayhi

Extraordinary Women from the Golden Age of Muslim Civilisation n.d. 1001inventions.com, http://www.1001inventions.com/womensday

Facts and figures: Leadership and political participation 2017, UN Women, http://www.unwomen.org/en/what-we-do/leadership-and-political-participation/facts-and-figures

Khan, S 2014, *Fatima al-Fihri: Founder of World's Very First University,* whyislam.org, https://www.whyislam.org/muslim-heritage/fatima-al-fihri-founder-of-worlds-very-first-university/

McCue, H 2008, *The Civil and Social Participation of Muslim Women in Australian Community Life,* Department of Immigration and Citizenship, https://www.dss.gov.au/sites/default/files/files/settle/multicultural_australia/participation-muslim-women.pdf

Raiza Sultana **2017, Wikipedia,** https://en.wikipedia.org/wiki/Razia_Sultana

Sadaf, M 2017, *Muslim Women and the History of Science,* aboutislam.com, http://aboutislam.net/science/science-tech/muslim-women-history-science

Shajar al-Durr 2018, Wikipedia, https://en.wikipedia.org/wiki/
Shajar_al-Durr

Sultan, S 1999, *Mirāth al-Mar'a wa-Qadiyyat al-Musāwa,* Dar Nahdat
Misr

[Then] Labana of Cordoba – Mathematician 2012, mosaicofmuslim-
women.com, https://mosaicofmuslimwomen.com/2012/02/
labana-of-cordoba/

The World's Women 2015: Trends and Statistics 2015, United Nations,
https://unstats.un.org/unsd/gender/chapter6/chapter6.html

Yahya, S 2017, *Rufaida Al-Aslamia – the first Muslim nurse,* msn-
news.com, https://www.msn.com/en-ae/news/middleeast/
rufaida-al-aslamia-%E2%80%93-the-first-muslim-nurse/
ar-BBz8Txw

Y, Dr. 2012, *Sameera Moussa: World-renowned Egyptian Nuclear
Scientist,* afrolegends.com, https://afrolegends.com/2012/08/06/
sameera-moussa-world-renowned-egyptian-nuclear-scientist/

Yurkiewicz, I 2012, *Study shows gender bias in science is
real. Here's why it matters,* Scientific American, https://
blogs.scientificamerican.com/unofficial-prognosis/
study-shows-gender-bias-in-science-is-real-heres-why-it-matters/

Zainab al Ghazali 2017, Wikipedia, https://en.wikipedia.org/wiki/
Zainab_al_Ghazali

Zubaidah bint Ja'far n.d. Wikipedia, https://en.wikipedia.org/wiki/
Zubaidah_bint_Ja%6ofar

About The Author

Kathryn Jones
Motivational Speaker, Author & Entrepreneur

Kathryn Jones is the author of *Step Up. Embrace The Leader Within*, a book dedicated to supporting Muslim women discover their inner leader and step up in every aspect of their lives.

She is the founder of the **Beautiful Muslimah Academy**, the annual **ME First Summit** and the **Great Ramadan Giveaway.** She is known internationally as the **Peaceful Parenting Coach,** as well as a **Business Performance Coach** for Muslim women who wish to build a six-figure business in twelve months. Her primary focus is on supporting Muslim women to step up and embrace the leader within themselves so they can take charge of their lives, rather than have life take charge of them.

Kathryn's mission in life is to make a difference in the world of Muslim women and lead them from oppression to success and purpose in life. She is particularly passionate about addressing the 'tough' subjects, such as depression, child abuse, domestic violence, bullying, abusive parenting and other topics that are often swept under the carpet. Although she would love to change the lives of every individual touched by these experiences, she realises that to fulfil this mission she needs other Muslim women to be successfully doing this work. To build a revolution of Muslim women coaching Muslim women, she established the annual ME First

Summit and her own online marketing program especially to fast track their success.

She loves to bust the stereotypes people have about Muslim women just by being herself and supporting other Muslim women to follow suit. It is possible for every Muslim woman to be a part of the solution by embracing the leader within themselves. Kathryn's program **Step Up: Leadership For Muslim Women** helps Muslim women take charge of their lives and live purposefully.

She also has a vision to build a Muslim parenting revolution where children are brought up with loving connection to their parents so that they meet their full emotional and intellectual potential to be strong and resilient leaders of the future.

This is also the key to successfully ending the issues such as abuse, addictions and mental illness. It all begins with **mastering your emotions** and Kathryn teaches how to do this through understanding the Inside Out Paradigm, the psychological paradigm that brings about effortless transformation, healthy psychology and inner peace.

Kathryn Jones is a mother of five children, a certified Parenting by Connection Instructor through Hand in Hand Parenting in the USA and a certified Inside Out Paradigm Coach. With a degree in IT and a Graduate Diploma of Teaching, Kathryn's thirteen years experience in the IT industry, both in technical, sales and marketing and managerial roles means she is able to help entrepreneurs in all aspects of building a business online, including the elusive 'technical stuff'.

Kathryn's websites:

www.BeautifulMuslimahAcademy.com
www.KathrynLJones.com

Email: Kathryn@kathrynljones.com

FREE Step Up Bonus

Assalamu Alaikum my beautiful sister in Islam.

Thank you for reading *Step Up. Embrace The Leader Within*.

I have another gift for you ...

This book was designed to be a reflective journey to understand self-leadership and to bring hope. Anything is possible for Allah, as He says in the Qur'an:

Verily, His command, when He intends a thing, is only that He says to it, 'Be!' – and it is! – Qur'an 36:82

We are also reminded that Allah will not burden us with more than we can manage in Chapter 2, Verse 286 of the Qur'an.

So whatever situation, condition, or predicament you find yourself in, you are OK!

If you left this book with only the message that you are OK, then it has been a success.

To make it even more successful for you I have added the reflection questions at the end of each chapter and turned these into a workbook and accompanying course. The link has been at the bottom of each chapter. It is:

www.StepUpBonus.com

For those who are serious about stepping up in their life, taking charge of their direction rather than being like a leaf blown in every direction by the wind, I have another special bonus for you … you may have already found it at the end of the online bonus course.

FREE Embrace The Leader Within Discovery Session where we will:

- Get clarity on what it is you are truly wanting out of your life, personally, spiritually and emotionally, so you have purpose and direction

- Discover what might be slowing you down, getting in the way or even stopping your from having that

- So you can leave the session feeling inspired, recharged and excited to embrace the leader within you.

The only condition is you complete the online course Step Up Bonus at www.StepUpBonus.com to be eligible. I will expect you to come to the session with an attempt at each reflection question in the workbook!

Details how you can book in can be found at the end of the course.

Can't want to speak to you soon!

With peace, love and blessings,

FREE training

Embracing The Leader Within

Leadership is an inside job. You can study all the courses, attend all the trainings in the world, but unless you embrace the leader within yourself it will not work out. This is all about becoming the leader of your own life rather than have life leading you. In this eye opening training you will uncover:

- How you can be a natural leader of yourself, your family and others around you with confidence

- How to say 'no', as well ask for what you want or need in a powerful, yet respectful manner that has the people close to you listening

- So you can live your life with inner peace, effortless patience and total resilience.

Essential learning for all Muslim women.

www.LeadershipForMuslimWomen.com

The Muslimah Coach

Should I just focus on coaching Muslim women? This dilemma is discussed over and over as Muslim women coaches doubt the potential of the Muslimah market. In this training I will reveal my secret to marketing to our sisters in Islam. You will learn:

- What is different about our niche and why it seems so hard to get sisters to join your coaching and programs

- Why standard marketing practises, even if they are followed perfectly, don't appear to work or convert as they do for those working in other niches

- The exact steps that you need to follow to sign up Muslim women and build a profitable and sustainable business.

Especially for Muslim women coaching Muslim women.

www.TheMuslimahCoach.com

Peaceful Parenting Secrets

In this powerful master class, you'll discover what is sabotaging your ability to remain calm and in charge in those stressful parenting moments so you can turn it around and:

- Stop Flying Off The Handle – and take charge of every challenge your children throw at you in a calm and collected way – and, on top of that, they actually listen to you

- Parent Peacefully – parenting no longer becomes a battle ground but is joyful, fun and loving, just like the Sunnah (way) of the Prophet (peace be upon him)

- Parent With Confidence – cast aside self-doubt, fear and anxiety about your children and never worry again about the attitudes and comments from others about your parenting!

Suitable for babies to teens and beyond!

www.PeacefulParentingSecrets.com

Engage Kathryn to Speak
at Your Next Event!

KATHRYN JONES

Kathryn's mission in life is to make a difference in the world of Muslim women and lead them from oppression to success and purpose in life. She is particularly passionate about addressing the 'tough' subjects such as depression, child abuse, domestic violence, bullying, abusive parenting and other topics that are often swept under the carpet. Although she would love to change the lives of every individual touched by these experiences, she realises that to fulfil this mission she needs other Muslim women to be successfully doing this work. To build a revolution of Muslim women coaching Muslim women she established the annual ME First Summit and her own online marketing program especially to fast track their success.

She loves to bust the stereotypes people have about Muslim women just by being herself and supporting other Muslim women to follow suit. It is possible for every Muslim woman to be a part of the solution by embracing the leader within them. Kathryn's program Step Up: Leadership For Muslim Women helps Muslim women take charge of their lives and live purposefully.

Kathryn is a sought after speaker on the following topics:

Embracing The Leader Within

Inspiration for Muslim women to step up into the best life they can lead with passion and purpose despite the oppression and challenges they face.

Muslim Women Living In The West

Targeting the specific challenges of being a Muslim woman, obvious as the 'other', as intolerance for Muslims grow in the West. Her struggles in the workplace, society and in bringing up children who want to belong.

Entrepreneurial-ship For Muslim Women

As the workplace becomes harder for Muslim women, more are seeking to work from home. This key talk is to inspire and encourage Muslim women to be strong & influential leaders in business.

Parenting For Paradise

We are all shepherds of our flock and the most important flock are our children. Understanding what is required to have our important work as parents accepted by Allah is critical to *Parenting For Paradise*.

To Engage Kathryn:

Email:
kathryn@kathrynljones.com
or visit
kathrynljones.com/speaker